fabulous
felted
hand-knits

fabulous felted hand-knits

wonderful wearables & home accents

Jane Davis

Lark Books

A Division of Sterling Publishing Co., Inc.
New York

Editor: Valerie Van Arsdale Shrader
Art Director: Tom Metcalf
Photographer: Stewart O'Shields
Photographer's Assistant: Katie Humphries
Cover Designer: Barbara Zaretsky
Illustrator: Jane Davis
Technical Consultant: Marilyn Hastings
Associate Art Director: Shannon Yokeley
Assistant Editor: Rebecca Guthrie
Editorial Assistance: Delores Gosnell
Editorial Interns: Janna Norton, Matthew M. Paden
Photography Intern: Nora Badr

The Library of Congress has cataloged the hardcover edition as follows:

Davis, Jane, 1959-
  Fabulous felted hand-knits : wonderful wearables & home accents / by Jane
Davis.
    p. cm.
  Includes index.
  ISBN 1-57990-560-9
  1. Knitting—Patterns. 2. Felting. I. Title.
TT825.D3826 2005
746.43'20432—dc22

2004023637

10 9 8 7 6 5 4 3 2 1

Published by Lark Books, A Division of
Sterling Publishing Co., Inc.
387 Park Avenue South, New York, N.Y. 10016

First Paperback Edition 2006
Text, illustrations, © 2005 Jane Davis
Photography © 2005 Lark Books

Distributed in Canada by Sterling Publishing,
c/o Canadian Manda Group, 165 Dufferin Street
Toronto, Ontario, Canada M6K 3H6

Distributed in the United Kingdom by GMC Distribution Services,
Castle Place, 166 High Street, Lewes, East Sussex, England BN7 1XU

Distributed in Australia by Capricorn Link (Australia) Pty Ltd.,
P.O. Box 704, Windsor, NSW 2756 Australia

If you have questions or comments about this book, please contact:
Lark Books, 67 Broadway, Asheville, NC 28801, (828) 253-0467

Manufactured in China

ISBN 13: 978-1-57990-560-6 (hardcover) 978-1-57990-957-4 (paperback)
ISBN 10: 1-57990-560-9 (hardcover) 1-57990-957-4 (paperback)

For information about custom editions, special sales, premium and corporate purchases, please contact Sterling Special Sales Department at 800-805-5489 or specialsales@sterlingpub.com.

contents

introduction

Getting knitwear to shrink and fuzz up into felt is a wonderful accident that has recently grown into a popular technique used to create contemporary knitwear. Knitters debate what to call this process, because to be honest, the term "felted knits" is a misnomer. Technically, *felting* is the process of working individual fibers together until they are matted into a fabric. In contrast, *fulling* is done when you take a knitted or woven piece and felt it. It's a fine line, but one that is distinct and is inevitably brought up at some point in many conversations about felting knitwear, with the purists and the not-so-purists at odds over terminology.

Name aside, then, how does this transformation happen? Fibers that are rubbed by constant use, or by intent, slowly tangle together until they become locked into a matted fabric. For centuries, felt was created on purpose to make firm clothing that was protective against cold wind and rain. By contrast, felting (or fulling, if you're a purist) might happen today as the result of an unfortunate mishap, when a precious hand-knit is ruined by a careless toss in the washer. But when the felting of your knitting is *intentional*, wondrous things can occur. To encourage this exciting new application of knitting, here are 30 fun projects to explore felting in a purposeful way. I've worked on different methods to begin and end a project as well as novel ways to add color, texture, and design. You'll find new project ideas, such as the mola-style rug pictured at the right, as well as classic silhouettes that incorporate wool's miraculous ability to transform into felt.

I've arranged this book to emphasize some of the great things you can do with felted knitting, beginning with a basics section to get you started. The first batch of projects are simple, including a lovely scarf that is just a long knitted rectangle with fringe made of I-cord. (There is a detail of this project below.) The chapter that follows demonstrates some ideas for combining felted knitting with regular knitting, such as the sweater jacket that takes advantage of the dense warmth of felting and combines it with the flexibility of traditional knitting.

There's a chapter that explores a little bit of embroidery—before *and* after felting the knitting—and there's beaded embroidery as well. In the chapter on cut-and-sew methods, you'll see that once you've felted your knitting, it's a fabric that can be sewn and worked like

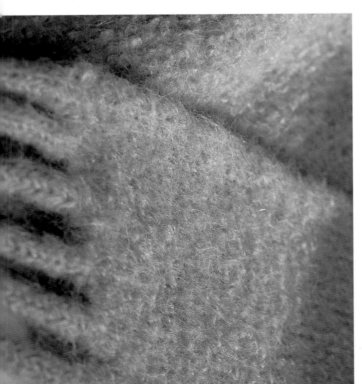

fleece to make anything from pillows to purses. Colorwork is the topic of another section, with everything from simple stripes to a Native American-style design. Variegated yarn used in a bag project adds more detail. Finally, for fun, there's a chapter on embellishing your knitting with novelty yarns that don't felt when they are thrown in the washer.

I hope these projects get your creative energy flowing so you take your knitting skills and try something new with felting. There is so much pleasure to be had in experimenting with an accident!

felting
basics

Let's get technical for a moment. Here's what actually happens during the felting process.

The only fibers that can be felted are from animals—sheep, goats, or rabbits, to name a few. An individual strand of animal hair is like a flexible stick made of protein, covered with a layer of scales called the *cuticle*. The scales are arranged like the shingles on the roof of a house, covering the hair from the base to the tip. Heat and moisture have an intriguing effect on animal hair; when it is in warm or hot water, the scales open up and fan away from the hair. If you add friction by rubbing the hairs against each other when the scales are open, they tangle together.

When the hair is in cold water, though, the scales close tightly to the hair and lock together, especially if friction is applied for a brief time. This is what causes the dense matted fabric created from felting. And long ago, feltmakers learned that the addition of soap to the hot water aids in the process by increasing the pH of the wool and speeding the swelling of the scales. Soap also lubricates the fibers, letting them felt more gently with less stress. So it's a pretty simple process, really. Take your knitting, wash it in warm water, rinse it in cool water, and let it dry.

This detail from the sweater project on page 45 illustrates the magic of felting. This is the same yarn, but it's felted in the bodice on the left and simply knitted in the sleeve on the right.

choosing
the right yarn

Remember that animal fibers can be felted, as long as the hair is covered with scales that are affected by heat and cold. This category includes wool from sheep and goats as well as fibers from other animals such as alpacas, angora rabbits, and camels. The degree of felting you achieve—whether your work retains stitch definition or not—is dependent on many factors. Some fibers are more apt to felt and/or felt much more quickly than others, for example, and different colored yarns may felt to varying degrees. Experimentation is always the key with this adventurous form of knitting.

These before-and-after swatches—all cast on 25 stitches and worked 25 rows—show the variation that exists when yarns are felted. The pink swatches were knit on 6mm (size 10 U.S.) needles, the others on 4.5mm (size 7 U.S.) needles.

Plant fibers and synthetic fibers *don't* felt. However, these are great yarns to use for some interesting effects in felted projects, and they can also help in controlling the outcome of the process. Blended yarns can be successfully felted depending on how much animal fiber is in the blend. If at least 50 percent of the content is animal fiber (such as 20 percent mohair, 30 percent wool, 50 percent acrylic), the yarn usually can be felted. Using a blended yarn can bring a new look to the finished piece, with little bits of unfelted fiber popping up randomly. On the other hand, the synthetic fiber might not even show depending on how the yarn was blended during the manufacturing process.

Many yarns from animal fibers are actually treated with chemicals to prevent felting, since up until recently felting your knitting has been considered a bad thing. So if you want to felt your knitting, it's important to use only yarns that *have not* been treated to make them washable. (Look for these designations on the yarn label.) You should also make a test swatch of your yarn or even a small easy project to see if it felts the way you hope it will. Sometimes the same brand of yarn will felt differently in one color than in another. This may be a problem…or it may not. It depends on the design of your project. If you only use a small amount of yarn that doesn't felt well, or if you use it evenly throughout the project, it can enhance the visual interest of the finished piece. Like felting itself, it may be another "mistake" that could be transformed into a design technique.

Though these novelty fibers won't felt, they can be used as decorative accents in your projects.

Do the Stitches Matter?

Stitch patterns often disappear during the felting process. That's why most felting projects are worked in stockinette stitch or garter stitch. These stitches felt a little differently from one other; garter stitch is already shorter and thicker than stockinette stitch, row for row, so it felts thicker and doesn't shrink as much lengthwise. Garter stitch can result in a nice textured pattern if it isn't felted completely.

It is possible to create some subtle effects and texture by using different stitches, however, and the amount you choose to felt your piece affects how visible the stitch pattern is. Increases and decreases help shape projects, but they also can be used in pattern repeats that show up in the finished item. The key is to make them dramatic rather than subtle, as you'll see in the scarf on page 104.

See how differently these stitches are affected by the felting process. The example on the top is garter stitch; on the bottom is stockinette stitch. Both are knit on 5.5mm (size 9 U.S.) needles, cast on 25 stitches and worked 25 rows.

The effect of lace patterns is usually lost in felted knitting, as you see in the photo below. By the very nature of felting, the open holes in the lacework felt together, with all the time spent concentrating on the work for naught. Sometimes you can preserve the appearance of lacework by felting your project less than you normally might, as suggested above.

The lovely effects created by intricate patterns tend to disappear when the piece is felted.

how well will it felt?

Felting is somewhat unpredictable, which keeps it interesting! The success of a felting project depends on many different elements in the process. Hard or soft water, the type and amount of soap you use, the water temperature, the length of agitation time, and even the type of agitation, are all factors in how much, how soon, and how smooth your knitwork will felt.

The yarn itself is of course a factor too. Because it's a natural fiber from animals, it might have developed properties based on the climate in the year before the animal was sheared, or perhaps the type of feed the animal ate while its coat grew. Because of these variables, you can't depend on a specific yarn from a specific company to felt a specific way every single time. Remember that it's always best to make a test swatch or a small project first to see what happens. Be sure to record the gauge and measurements of the piece before *and* after felting so you can get the same results when you begin your larger project.

Here's a before-and-after shot of the coaster project. The completed felted piece is lying on the top of the original knitted piece; note how beautifully this yarn has felted. Knit on 6.5mm (size 10½ U.S.) needles, cast on 18 stitches, and worked for 26 rows in stockinette stitch.

The armholes in this vest had additional hand felting done to make sure they wouldn't ravel.

If you were making traditional felt from wool roving (a thick rope of wool fibers), you would need to felt it thoroughly so the fibers lock together into a fabric. It's all or nothing. With knitwear, you've already completed the process of getting the fibers—the yarn—into a fabric that's not going to fall apart. After you've done that, you have a lot of freedom in deciding to which degree you'd like to felt your knitting. This is part of the great appeal of this process, because you choose the degree of "feltedness" that you achieve. Some like to have their knits fully felted so that the knitting stitches don't show. Look at the bodice section of the sweater jacket on page 45 for an example. Others like to have stitch definition still visible. Yet another option is to have some of the project felted more in one place and less in another. In the vest shown above, the armhole openings are hand felted much more than the rest of the piece so you don't need to finish them with a facing.

In addition to the degree of felting you achieve, another entirely personal issue is which side of the felted knitting to use in your project. In many cases, the project is worked in stockinette stitch and the knit side will normally be used as the right side. With fully felted knits, you often can't distinguish one side from the other. However, in the projects in the cut-and-sew section, you have the option of adding textural contrast by using the knit side of some pieces and the purl side of other pieces. So look at both sides of your felting and see if there are any possibilities there. Remember that you can also create interesting opportunities for texture by either felting your knitting thoroughly, so the stitches disappear, or by felting it less, to retain some stitch definition.

At the top, note the different textures of the knit side (left) and the purl side (right) of the felted swatches. They are knit on 4.5mm (size 7 U.S.) needles, cast on 25 stitches and worked 25 rows in stockinette stitch.

preparing
to felt

Making a swatch is an important beginning for your project. It shows you how your yarn behaves in the felting method you have chosen, how long it takes to felt it, how much more the length of the knitting felts in relation to the width—which can be substantial!—and what texture your finished work will have. This differs from yarn to yarn and process to process. Swatches are a great way to test out new ideas, such as trying two different types of yarn together to see if they will felt to the same size, or seeing how much a novelty yarn will show up when knitted along with a wool yarn. If you don't like the idea of making swatches you won't use, plan a small easy project as a test, maybe one of the gift bags on page 32. Then you can determine how your yarn will handle for your actual project and calculate how much you will need.

A small piece like this surprise bag can serve as a swatch in preparation for a larger project. It is shown both felted and nonfelted here; this bag is worked on 5.5mm (size 9 U.S.) needles, cast on 40 stitches, for 100 rows.

Can I Do It?

Of course you can! The knitting skills you will need for the projects in this book range from beginning to advanced. The projects with simple shaping, such as the hat on page 55, can be completed by someone with advanced beginning to intermediate knitting skills. Several of the projects require a little stronger background in specific areas of knitting, such as two-color knitting.

But since many of the projects are made from simple rectangles, they are perfect for all skill levels, especially those who are just learning to knit. Because your stitches usually disappear in the felting process, a beginning knitter doesn't have to worry about uneven knitting stitches as much as in traditional knitting projects. It's a great way to practice knitting and experiment with felting.

What a swatch *doesn't* show is how the actual project will respond to the felting process in the washing machine. The weight of a large, wet piece can alter the shape. Projects that are long to begin with, such as scarves and handles on bags, can actually stretch *longer* in the washing machine rather than shrinking shorter as you would expect. A project might also pull toward the outer corners and shrink more in the center. So it's important to carefully monitor larger projects during the felting process to avoid any major surprises.

basting
is important

When you throw your knitting into the washing machine, it's a chancy thing. You don't know if it's going to shrink exactly the way you want it to, or get caught on the agitator or another piece of knitting and stretch way out of shape. I've noticed that pieces felted in the machine seem to shrink at the middle and stretch at the edges. This tendency is great for a hat because you can knit it like a tall cylinder, without any increases on the sides. Then, when you put it in the washer, the hat magically flares out at the edges and you have the perfect cloche. I'm not sure why this happens, but it's a nice design tool for hats.

With most other projects, though, this tendency to stretch at the edges is certainly not an asset. To make a vest or to felt your knitting into a flat rectangle, you need to prepare the edges so they're stable in the machine. You can knit fewer stitches at the edge of your piece, for example, but I rely heavily on basting the edges with cotton crochet thread. Another alternative is to use cotton yarn to work a few rows along the edges that you don't want to distort; this keeps them from flaring. (The rows of cotton yarn are removed later.) You can also crochet along the open edges or baste the opening closed as was done in many of the projects. Each set of project instructions will offer specific directions about basting.

The flap of this eyeglass case is basted and the project is ready to felt.

Basting stitches help create the shape of this clutch.

Another technique you might find useful (and fun) is to use basting stitches as a design tool. In the clutch shown above I basted the opening of the purse to the back; it stayed the same size in the middle and flared out at the edges! To make sure that the hat on page 41 ended up the proper size, I measured the cotton crochet thread to the finished hat size and wove it in and out along the base of the hat (not the brim). Then I threw it in the washer, knowing the hat wouldn't stretch out of shape—at least in that place.

Lastly, to get two items that are knit identically to end up the same size and shape, it works wonders to baste them together along their edges. This handy technique is used in several projects. The pieces won't felt to one another, even though it seems that they might.

Choosing Cotton Thread for Basting

The cotton thread you use for basting needs to be strong, smooth, and thin enough so it won't leave huge holes when it's removed. I like to use size 10 cotton crochet thread and a tapestry needle; this size pulls out easily. I make my basting stitches about $\frac{1}{4}$–$\frac{3}{8}$" (6–10mm) long, depending on the size of the project, and I use an off-white or white crochet thread so I can find the stitches easily when removing them. If you find you have visible holes when you pull out the thread, you can rub the felting a little and they will usually disappear.

learning
to felt

Even though the basic transformation from knitwear to felted knitwear happens because of a known physical change, there are many different approaches to achieve a desired result. Techniques vary in the use of water temperatures, duration of friction, and rinsing procedures, but here are the methods that I used for the projects in this book. They work!

hand
felting

The easiest way to felt something small is to do it with your own two hands over the kitchen sink. The projects in this book that specify "hand felt" were produced using this method.

Place a large shallow bowl in (or near) the sink and fill it with very hot or boiling water (about 1qt/1L). Add a small amount (about ¼tsp/1mL) of liquid dish soap (as opposed to dish detergent) and stir gently. Place the knitted item in the bowl and let it soak for a few minutes. In the meantime, place another bowl in the sink and fill it with cold water and ice cubes (about ½qt/500mL of water and a dozen ice cubes). The amount of water doesn't matter so much, but the warm water should be very warm and the cold water very cold. This helps the process move along faster.

When the knitting feels very wet and heavy because it has absorbed as much water as it can, take it in your hands and rub vigorously. (Be sure the water's not hot enough to burn your hands before you begin. Rubber gloves may be in order.) If you're making something in the shape of a ball, roll it around between your hands. If you're felting a small flat shape, rub back and forth in one direction, then change direction and continue

Hand felting is a simple procedure using hot water and friction.

Be sure to constantly check the progress of your felting, especially if you are making a garment where fit is critical.

machine
felting

Most of the projects in this book were machine felted. This is by far the easiest way to felt large items, though you give up a lot of control since you can't see it during the entire process. You also run the risk of having a strap get caught in the machine and stretch out rather than shrink. Even worse, you may forget to check on your project and wind up with a teeny tiny vest instead of one that should fit you. I'm writing from experience here, having had to re-knit and redesign several large projects for this book! Here are some tips.

1 Use liquid dish soap (not detergent). It really helps the water soak into the fibers, which in turn causes them to open up and mix together so they felt better.

2 Put a white canvas bag (or similar item) in with the knitting so you create more friction than the machine alone can provide. This also helps your project felt faster.

3 Don't ever put anything other than a light-colored, nonpilling material in the washer when felting your knitting. Terry cloth towels will fuzz and the lint will permanently work into your projects. Blue jeans or any colored fabric can discolor your knitwear, especially if your project is made with light-colored yarn. I do put like colors of knitwear together and felt them at the same time, but only if I'm absolutely sure I won't mind if some of one color ends up in the other project.

rubbing. After a few minutes, dip the knitting in the ice water and continue rubbing. The felting might happen immediately, or you may need to dip back and forth from the hot to the cold. Continue to work the knitting until it shrinks and fuzzes up as much as you want, then gently rinse any remaining soap out of it in cool running water. Roll the felted knitting up tightly in a terry cloth towel to remove as much water as possible, then take it from the towel and manipulate it into the finished shape.

Let it dry in a warm place, usually overnight. This can be on top of the dryer or in a warm oven. If you use the oven, turn it on to 250 °F/122 °C, let it warm up, and then turn it off. Place your felted knitting on a dry towel on a cookie sheet and leave it in the oven overnight. You can also let your felted knitting dry outside in the shade on a warm day, but avoid drying it in direct sunlight just in case the color in the yarn isn't fade-resistant. It might take a while to dry.

How Loose or How Tight?

Most felting instructions advise you to use very large needles so your project is quite loose, open, and flimsy compared to standard knitted fabric. This is suggested so the fibers will have more room to rub together and will felt better. I've found that this is really not as important as it seems. Projects in this book were knitted both loosely and not so loosely, and frankly they all felted about the same. In my experience, it's the amount of felting done that determines the density of the project rather than the initial gauge. Below are examples of swatches knitted with different sized needles, and they have all felted just fine, though they are different sizes.

These swatches were all knit with the same yarn, at different gauges, and all felted successfully. The swatches were cast on 25 stitches and worked 25 rows. At the top, 9mm (size 13 U.S.) needles; at the bottom left, 3.75mm (size 5 U.S.) needles; and at the bottom right, 5.5mm (size 9 U.S.) needles.

4) You can put your knitting in the dryer too, to help it felt some more. I *only* do this with items that don't need to be a specific size, like bags and purses. It's usually too risky for wearables such as gloves, mittens, and vests, unless they are extremely oversized and need to shrink as much as possible. Even so, don't walk away from the dryer, and take a peek every few minutes! (If you find that you're often using your dryer for felting, be sure to check the lint filter and don't allow the fuzz to build up in your machine, posing a fire hazard.)

5) Lastly, and most importantly, *check on your project*. Do this as often as every three to five minutes if it's a wearable that won't fit if it shrinks too much. If you're felting a large or unusually shaped piece, you may need to take it out and rearrange it if your project gets twisted up in one position; this might cause it to felt only on one side or perhaps stretch out awkwardly. Until you have done machine felting a few times you won't be able to adequately judge how long to let it stay in the washer.

Remember that experimentation is the key to felting. Sometimes "surprises" happen even if you do feel that you know how long to leave it in the washer. Then you'll have to figure out what to make from your "surprise."

using
the machine

So with all that in the way of introduction, here is how I felt in the washing machine.

I put the knitting, a white canvas bag, and about 1Tbsp/15mL of liquid dish soap in the machine. I set the machine for a hot wash and a cold rinse using the lowest water level available; the low water level allows for more friction, thus quicker felting. After the washer gets going, I check it partway through the wash cycle when it's still soapy and full of water, and then right after all the water has spun out before the rinse cycle begins. I peek at it again during the rinse cycle, and yet again at the end of the rinse cycle. If at any time during these checks it looks like it's done, I'll skip to the spin cycle to stop the process.

If the project happens to felt quickly at the beginning of the process when there's still soap in the piece, I'll take it to my sink and rinse it out under cool running water. Then I return it to the machine to spin, but only after the washer has completed the rinse cycle so I'm not putting the knitting back into soapy water. Sometimes I go through the whole cycle and the piece still isn't felted, or it's not felted enough. Then I start the procedure all over again. Occasionally I'll put it through the dryer, letting the project get completely dry, and then through the washer again to get better results.

note

If you've felted before and used other instructions, you've probably noticed that I don't put my knitting in a mesh bag before it goes in the washing machine. Maybe I shouldn't admit it, but I've found that my knitting felts much better loose in the machine without being inside the bag. When I tried that method, the knitting got so bundled up I had to constantly take it out and rearrange it so it would felt evenly. But a mesh bag does help control the amount of lint in your machine, and I *was* concerned about the amount of loose fibers left inside the washer. I decided to risk it anyway, knowing I might be calling a repairman to fix my machine that wasn't draining properly with the accumulation of excess lint. In actual practice, it never happened in over a hundred washings, so I'm going to continue to felt without the mesh bag. If you're uncomfortable with my method, do place your knitting in a mesh laundry bag to keep lint from building up in your machine. Your knitting will felt; you just may need to check it more often.

preparing
to dry

Once your piece has felted to your satisfaction, it doesn't necessarily mean you're done fiddling with it. There's often still plenty of room for adjustments, and you can greatly improve the finished appearance of your project with a little attention at this stage. The first thing to be concerned with is shaping your piece. The felting process can distort the corners or stretch *here* when you want it to stretch *there*. Some things might felt into a shape or size that isn't right for the project; an example of this is the scarf on page 57, also seen on the opposite page. After this scarf has finished felting, you'll need to pull and stretch it longer and thinner so it's not as thick, bulky, and short as it was when it came out of the washer. Small projects like the coasters on page 26 are easily adjusted into close-to-perfect squares and will then dry in the proper shape. If you left the coasters exactly as they came out of the washer, they would be warped and uneven looking. Much like in regular knitting, blocking does take some time and effort, but the process is well worth it to make your finished work look polished.

You may want to use a hairbrush as a finishing touch, too. Brushing the surface may help your piece look a little more felted, if you feel it's necessary. (You can also use a brush after the piece is dry to eliminate pills and make the surface softer and smoother.)

Basting stitches are another issue. Do you take

A little bit of simple shaping is usually all that's needed before you let your pieces dry.

The basting stitches—actually a chain of crochet stitches—are being removed in preparation for knitting the cuffs onto these mittens.

them out when the project is wet, or let it dry and then remove them? That depends greatly on the project and how the basting stitches were used. In the hat on page 41, I put the basting stitches in to size the hat and left them in permanently so the hat retained its shape. In the bag on page 98, I took the basting stitches out while the piece was still wet so I could pull it open and make sure the top edge was smooth and even. Use the latter technique for any project you've folded in half and basted together that needs smooth edges.

Bits of wool that have come out of the yarn in the felting process tend to ball up and migrate to the inside corners of the projects. Be sure to check all the nooks and crannies and remove all the loose wool to aid in the shaping and drying of your project.

Use the same methods discussed with hand felting (page 15) to dry your project.

Some items, such as this scarf, will require some stretching into shape while they are still wet.

It's an Adventure!

Without innovation (and failure), we wouldn't have electricity, telephones, novelty yarns, or felted knitting. The process of felting knitwear sprang from experimentation, and the key to it is to have fun! So don't be afraid to try different combinations of yarns and stitches. Then, when something unexpected happens, try to incorporate it into a successful project, even though the result may be quite different from what you were planning to do in the first place.

---

good
felting gone bad

Sometimes disaster strikes. If your project didn't felt enough, you can always work to felt it again. But when it's felted *more* than you want or has become too small, it's very difficult and often impossible to correct. Sometimes you can stretch a piece to the size you want while it's still wet, as the scarf you see above, but it's really just best to monitor your knitting carefully during the felting process. Don't automatically throw out your mistakes, either. You can cut them up and use them for coasters, or make small pincushions or bags. They will be beautiful with the addition of a little embroidery or a favorite charm. Felted pieces might be used under furniture to protect the floor or to wipe clean a message board. You can cut a piece to fit under your sewing machine when you put it on a table or make it into a case for your sewing needles or scissors. The possibilities are endless.

taking
care of your felt

Once you've felted your knitting, you need to treat it like any of your other fine knits or delicate washables. This is especially true for any projects that combine felted and nonfelted elements. If you throw your felted knitting in the washer and dryer it's sure to felt and shrink some more. To preserve the size and shape of your project, it will need to be hand washed, dry cleaned, or machine-washed in cold water on the gentle cycle. After washing, lay your items flat to dry.

using
this book

In addition to what you've learned in this chapter, be sure to read the introductions to each project section for more specific information about knitting and felting techniques. Each section offers something unique; for example, the Cut and Sew section lends a new twist when you use the felted knitting as a fabric and then complete the projects on your sewing machine. Each and every project in the book presents a new opportunity to enjoy this exciting form of knitting.

P.S. If you need to review basic knitting techniques before you begin, turn to the Glossary of Techniques on page 119.

tips
for success

Here are some last-minute reminders before you get started with the projects.

the design phase

Always make a test swatch to felt an untried yarn before beginning a major project.

When choosing stitches for your felted knitting, remember that dramatic techniques survive the process better than the subtle ones.

The looseness of your knitting doesn't matter as much as the amount your project is felted.

the knitting phase

Larger projects tend to stretch at the edges and they need some kind of treatment before felting, such as basting. Another strategy is to knit at the beginning or end of your project for several rows using a non-felting yarn, such as cotton, and remove the stitches after the project has been felted. (You can then knit an edging with the felting yarn.) Generally, you don't need to baste small projects.

Basting can also be used to set the finished size of a project (such as a hat) before felting, because the nonfelting yarn maintains the proper size.

the washing phase

Add liquid dish soap to the wash water to help open up the scales so the fibers felt more quickly.

Always check on your project periodically throughout the felting process.

Don't ever put a lint-producing item such as a terry cloth towel in the washer with your felting project. You'll never be able to remove all the bits of lint. But perhaps you'll intentionally include the lint to explore a new felting technique? Hmm....

If your project didn't felt enough, you can always put it through the process again to felt it some more. But if you felt it too much? You're stuck with what you've got.

You can felt your project a little or a lot—it's up to you—with the following two exceptions. When preparing for a cut-and-sew project, you need to fully felt the knitting so it won't fray. And when you're felting with novelty yarn, don't agitate the project so much that the novelty yarn is damaged (chenille is especially vulnerable).

the drying phase

Blocking and shaping your project when it's still wet can have a huge effect on how the piece looks when it's dry, so take the necessary time to put the finishing touches on your project.

simple

These easy-to-knit rectangles felt up into fun, functional items you can use and enjoy. Their relatively small size and simple construction allow you to learn a lot about the process of felting.

Starting with a basic square, you'll discover that a felted piece shrinks more in length than in width. You may also find that the yarn you choose for your project felts differently than the yarn used in this book. You'll learn how stripes change from the original knitted piece to the fuzzy, color-blended, felted project.

Basting before felting teaches you how to prepare projects so they maintain their shape. Cutting a buttonhole may seem daunting at first, but you'll find that the knitting will stay locked in place by the stitching around the opening. The scarf, with its I-cord fringe, is a great introduction to working on a larger piece because you'll prepare the edges with cotton yarn. Then, you'll monitor the felting process carefully to protect the dangly fringe.

Finally, you'll get to have fun with bags. Shape them in a number of different ways or add details like I-cord handles. Any of these projects will introduce you to the wonders of felting, along with some of its little quirks.

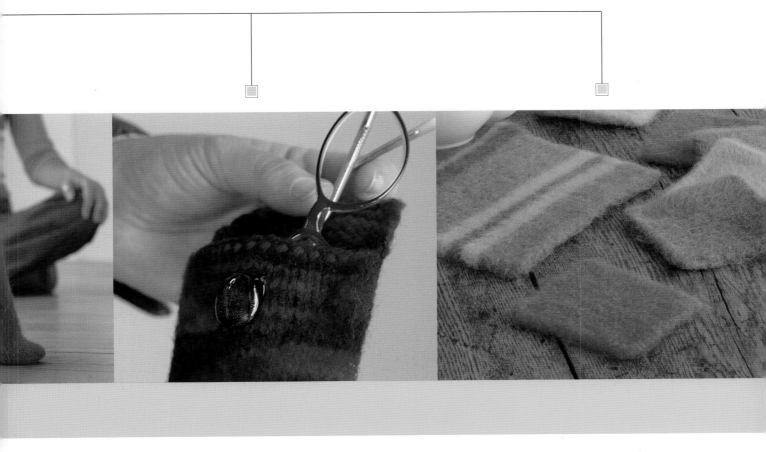

experience level
easy ●

All you have to do is knit two easy rectangles, throw them in the washer, and see

what happens! You'll see that the length shrinks more than the width, and you'll

be able to practice pulling the finished pieces into equal-sized squares.

finished measurements

before felting
  Approx 6 x 9"/15 x 23cm

after felting
  Approx 5"/13cm square

yarn

Approx total: 220yd/201m wool
medium weight yarn

materials

Knitting needles: 5.5mm (size 9 U.S.)
or size to obtain gauge

Polyester fiberfill

A piece of stiff cardboard or plastic, approx
5"/13cm square

Sewing needle and thread to match yarn color

gauge before felting

16 sts and 20 rows = 4"/10cm in
Stockinette Stitch
Always take time to check your gauge.

pattern stitch

Stockinette Stitch

INSTRUCTIONS (make two)

CO 24 sts. Work in St st for 45 rows, BO,
weave in ends.

felting

Felt in the washer until fully felted and square
(or almost square). Pull the pieces into shape if
necessary and dry flat.

assembly

Place the two pieces WS tog. Sew three sides
tog, insert cardboard or plastic in the bottom
and stuff with polyester fiberfill; the pincushion
should have a slightly concave top. Stitch
closed the remaining side.

this project was knit with

Harrisville Designs' *New England Knitters
Highland*, 100% virgin wool, worsted weight,
3.5oz/100g = approx 200yd/183m per ball,
1 ball of color #7919

spicy
coasters and hot pad

Here's a practical project that everyone in the house can enjoy using. The hot colors are perfect for summertime, but these handy items would also look great in fall colors or holiday red and green.

finished measurements

before felting
   Coasters: Approx 6 x 7"/15 x 18cm
   Hot Pad: Approx 11½ x 18¾"/29 x 48cm
after felting
   Coasters: Approx 4½"/11cm square
   Hot Pad: Approx 10 x 14½"/25 x 37cm

yarn

Approx total: 330yd/300m wool bulky weight yarn

Color A: 110yd/100m in green

Color B: 110yd/100m in yellow

Color C: 110yd/100m in melon

materials

Knitting needles: 6.5mm (size 10½ U.S.) *or size to obtain gauge*

Tapestry needle

gauge before felting

12 sts and 16 rows = 4"/10cm in Stockinette Stitch

Always take time to check your gauge.

pattern stitch
Stockinette Stitch

INSTRUCTIONS

coasters (make two in A, two in B, and two in C)

CO 18 sts. Work in St st for 26 rows, BO. Weave in ends.

hot pad

With A, CO 36 sts. Working in St st throughout, work 8 rows in A, 4 rows in B, 2 rows in C, 4 rows in B, 15 rows in A, 4 rows in C, 2 rows in B, 4 rows in C, 15 rows in A, 4 rows in B, 2 rows in C, 4 rows in B, 8 rows in A, BO. Weave in ends.

felting

Felt in the washer until the coasters are square (or almost square). Pull into shape and let dry.

this project was knit with

Reynolds Yarns' *Lopi*, 100% virgin wool, bulky weight, 3.5oz/100g = approx 110yd/100m per skein

(A) 1 skein, color #212

(B) 1 skein, color #213

(C) 1 skein, color #104

experience level

easy ●

This little case is a great way to display your favorite accent bead or button. The rich hand-dyed variegated yarn makes this a special holder for your favorite reading glasses.

finished measurements

before felting
Approx 4 x 7½"/10 x 19cm (with flap closed)
after felting
Approx 3 x 6½"/8 x 17cm (with flap closed)

yarn

Approx total: 250yd/228m wool medium weight yarn in variegated shades

materials

Knitting needles: 5.5mm (size 9 U.S.)
or size to obtain gauge
Cotton crochet thread
Tapestry needle
⅝"/2cm button
Needle and sewing thread to match yarn color
Cotton floss to match yarn color

gauge before felting

16 sts and 24 rows = 4"/10cm in Stockinette Stitch
Always take time to check your gauge.

pattern stitch

Stockinette Stitch

INSTRUCTIONS

CO 16 sts and work in St st for 16"/48cm (approx 95 rows).

Continuing in St st, dec 1 st ea end ea RS row until there are 2 sts left, k2tog, BO, weave in ends. Fold knitting in half 7½"/19cm from the beg row and sew side seams. Using the cotton crochet thread, baste the opening closed, stitching the flap down onto the front of the case.

felting

Felt in the washer, checking occasionally. Remove the basting thread when the felting is finished. Pull the case into shape if necessary and dry flat.

finishing

Sew the button to the front of the case with the sewing needle and thread. Cut a slit in the flap to fit the button. Stitch around the opening in buttonhole stitch, using the floss.

this project was knit with

Mountain Colors' *4/8's Wool*, 100% wool, worsted weight, 4oz/112g = approx 250yd/228m per skein, 1 skein of color Flathead Cherry

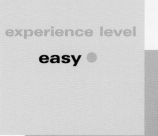
simple fringed scarf

Once you have tried your hand at felting small projects, you'll be ready for something larger. This simple design recalls the warmth of thick stadium blankets with their fringed edges. Crocheting along the sides before felting ensures the sides of the scarf will felt evenly with the center.

finished measurements

before felting
   Approx 12 x 90"/30 x 229cm (includes
   6"/15cm fringe at each end)

after felting
   Approx 8¾ x 76"/22 x 193cm (includes
   5½"/14cm fringe at each end)

yarn

Approx total: 756yd/690m wool fine weight yarn

materials

Knitting needles: 4.5 mm (size 7 U.S.)
or size to obtain gauge

Two 3.25mm (size 3 U.S.) dpn for the I-cord

Cotton yarn, sport or worsted weight

4.25mm or 5mm (size G or H U.S.) crochet hook

Tapestry needle

gauge before felting

20 sts and 24 rows = 4"/10cm in
Stockinette Stitch
Always take time to check your gauge.

pattern stitch

Stockinette Stitch

INSTRUCTIONS

With the larger needles, CO 60 sts. Work in St st for 460 rows, or until piece measures about 78"/198cm. Place sts on holder.

i-cord fringe

Pick up 4 sts from the holder on one of the dpn and work I-cord for 40 rows, BO. Cut the yarn to about 8"/20cm, thread with the tapestry needle and pass through rem sts. Weave in end. Rep for each group of 4 sts across the row. Make I-cord fringe on the other end of the scarf by picking up sts along the CO end of the scarf.

felting

Slipstitch along the sides of the scarf with the cotton yarn and hook. Let the fringe hang loose.

Felt in the washer until the scarf reaches the desired size and is well matted, but the stitches are still visible. Check the scarf often to make sure it hasn't become tangled. Remove the cotton yarn. Pull the scarf into shape if necessary and dry flat.

this project was knit with

Dale of Norway's *Tiur*, 60% mohair/40% pure new wool, sport weight, 1.75oz/50g = approx 126yd/115m per ball, 6 balls of color Light Green #8533

These elegant gift bags are great projects to use for experiments in felting. All are simple rectangles, folded in half and sewn together at the sides, but shaped in different ways. You can add stripes, use variegated yarn, embellish, and otherwise try out new ideas—all with a simple knitted rectangle.

finished measurements

before felting
   Red: Approx 4¼ x 13½"/11 x 34cm
   Orange: Approx 7½ x 14"/19 x 36cm
   Purple: Approx 10 x 17½"/25 x 44cm
after felting and shaping
   Red: Approx 3¼ x 5"/8 x 13cm
   Orange: Approx 6½ x 7"/17 x 18cm
   Purple: Approx 9½ x 7"/24 x 18cm

yarn

Approx total: 590yd/539m wool worsted weight yarn

materials

Knitting needles: 5.5mm (size 9 U.S.)
or size to obtain gauge
Tapestry needle
3"/8cm diameter drinking glass
30"/76cm of decorative cord
1 shoelace
6"/15cm balloon
Two 5.5mm (size 9 U.S.) dpn for the handles
Cotton crochet thread

gauge before felting

13 sts and 23 rows = 4"/10cm in Stockinette Stitch
Always take time to check your gauge.

pattern stitch

Stockinette Stitch

INSTRUCTIONS
for the Red Bag

Using A and 5.5mm (size 9 U.S.) needles, CO 14 sts. Work in St st for 80 sts, BO, weave in ends.

assembly

Fold in half so the bag is 6¾"/17cm long. Sew the side seams with the wool yarn.

felting

Felt in the washer until the bag is about 3"/8cm wide. While the bag is still wet, slide the glass inside and pull the bottom of the bag until it fits snugly around the glass. Adjust the top and sides of the bag so they are even. Let dry on the glass.

INSTRUCTIONS
for the Orange Bag

Using B and 5.5mm (size 9 U.S.) needles, CO 30 sts. Work in St st for 80 rows, BO, weave in ends.

assembly

Fold in half so the bag is 7"/18cm long. Sew the side seams. Turn the bag inside out and backstitch across the corners of the bottom of the bag as shown in figure 1. Weave in ends. Turn the bag right side out. Weave the shoelace in and out around the top of the bag, 4 rows from the top edge and 4 sts apart. (You'll need to insert the shoelace a few stitches closer together at the front to have both ends of it on the right side [the outside] of the bag.) Pull the shoelace so the bag is gathered tightly at the opening. Tie the ends together.

The felted project at the right doesn't vary much from the knitted version at the left; inserting an inflated balloon while this project dried helped preserve its size and shape.

felting

Felt in the washer. While the bag is still wet, untie the shoelace, blow up and tie the balloon, then slide the balloon inside the bag. Pull the shoelace tight and tie it again. Adjust the top and sides of the bag so they're even. Let the bag dry. Remove the balloon and replace the shoelace with a decorative ribbon or cord.

INSTRUCTIONS
for the Purple Bag

body

Using C and 5.5mm (size 9 U.S.) needles, CO 40 sts. Work in St st for 100 rows, BO, weave in ends.

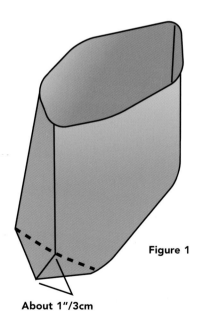

Figure 1

About 1"/3cm

This photo illustrates the amount of shrinkage you can expect from the yarn used in this project.

handles (make two)

Beg with an 8"/20cm tail (you'll sew the handle to the bag with this later), CO 3 sts on dpn. Work 40 rows of I-cord. Cut the yarn to 8"/20cm. Use the tapestry needle to weave the yarn through the last 3 sts. Set aside.

assembly

Fold the rectangle in half WS tog so the bag is 8 ¾"/22cm long. Sew one of the side seams, beginning at the top edge, working to 3"/8cm from the fold. Flatten the fold and sew the bottom edges together as shown in figure 2. Repeat for the other side seam. Using the tails on the I-cord handles, sew the handles to the top edge of the bag, 12 sts from each side seam. Weave in ends. Using the cotton thread, baste the bag opening shut.

felting

Felt in the washer. While the bag is still wet, remove the cotton thread. Adjust the top and sides of the bag so they are even. Let the bag dry flat.

these projects were knit with

Harrisville Designs' *New England Knitters Highland*, 100% virgin wool, worsted weight, 3.5oz/100g = approx 200yd/183m per ball

(A) 1 ball, color Red #2

(B) 1 ball, color Poppy #65

Brown Sheep's *Lamb's Pride*, 85% wool/15% mohair, worsted weight, 4oz/113g = approx 190yd/173m per ball

(C) 1 ball, color Amethyst #M-62

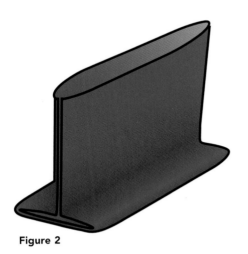

Figure 2

texture

Combining felted knitting with standard knitting is a great way to get the best of both worlds. You'll have dense warmth in some sections and stretchy flexibility in others. Slippers are the perfect project for this category, with a foot section that's warm and stable and a cuff that's elastic to hug the ankle. How about a hat that holds its shape when felted, yet the band around it stretches to fit—and can be changed to suit your mood? Mittens keep more cold weather out when they're felted but stay on your hands snugly when the cuffs are knitted without felting. A

sweater jacket has a cozy felted bodice, but it has a more comfortable fit with standard knitted sleeves. The remaining project in this group is a mesh bag with a felted bottom to protect its contents.

All of these projects involve knitting after the felting is done yet present different techniques to achieve the same goal. The processes include knitting a few rows in cotton yarn, casting on into a cotton yarn chain stitch, or sewing the finished knitting to the felted item.

fireside slippers

Interesting to make and warm to wear, these slipper socks are a great way to get your "feet wet" with some different felting techniques. You get to baste before felting, machine felt, cut the felted fabric, and hand felt, too. The knitted cuff is sewn to the felted section and the finished piece is in turn sewn to the leather bottom.

finished measurements

before felting
  Foot Section: Approx 5½ x 13"/14 x 33cm

after felting
  Slipper: Approx 4½ x 10"/11 x 25cm
  (Women's size medium)

yarn

Approx total: 600yd/549m wool medium weight yarn

Color A: 200yd/183m in red

Color B: 200yd/183m in gold

Color C: 200yd/183m in orange

materials

Knitting needles: 9mm (size 13 U.S.) dpn *or size to obtain gauge*

Women's fleece-lined slipper bottoms, size medium

Tapestry needle

Cotton crochet thread

Stitch marker

gauge before felting

10 sts and 13 rows = 4"/10cm in Stockinette Stitch

Always take time to check your gauge.

pattern stitches

Stockinette Stitch

K2, P2 Rib Stitch

INSTRUCTIONS (make two)

Using two strands of A held tog as one, CO 6 sts.

Rows 1, 3, 5, and 7: K into front and back of 1st st, k to last st, k into front and back of last st—8, 10, 12, 14 sts.

Row 2 and all wrong side rows: P.

Rows 8–42: Work in St st.

Row 43: K 7 sts, cut yarn to 18"/46cm and graft rem sts tog, working from the 2 center sts to the ends.

Weave in ends. Use the cotton thread to baste the bottoms of the slippers to one another along the edges as in figure 1.

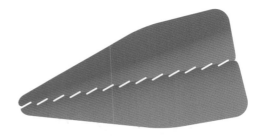

Figure 1

felting

Felt in the washer until the slipper bottoms fit the feet. Remove the cotton thread. Cut a 3"/8cm opening for your foot, beg at the top corner of the fold at the heel end as in figure 2. Hand felt the opening so it's completely felted throughout. Set aside to dry.

Figure 2

cuff

With B, holding 2 strands tog as 1, CO 32 sts over 3 or 4 dpn, pm.

Rnds 1–3: Working in the round, *k2, p2. Rep from *.

Rnds 4–7: Change one B to C, rep pat.

Rnds 8–11: Change rem B to C, rep pat.

Rnds 12–15: Change one C to A, rep pat.

Rnds 16–19: Change rem C to A, rep pat.

finishing

Sew rem row of the cuff to the opening in the foot that you cut and felted. Sew slipper foot to slipper bottom using buttonhole st.

this project was knit with

Harrisville Designs' *New England Knitters Highland*, 100% virgin wool, worsted weight, 3.5oz/100g = approx 200yd/183m per ball

(A) 1 ball, color Red #2

(B) 1 ball, color Poppy #65

(C) 1 ball, color Gold #4

white summer hat

experience level
easy ●

This is a fun and easy project that you can make in a day and change to fit any season.

The hat is knit from the center out. You'll baste with cotton thread to set the finished hat

size, so all you have to do is felt the hat until it shrinks down to the size you've already

set. The band is pinned in place so you can change it to suit your mood.

finished measurements

before felting
  Approx 13"/33cm from center to rim
after felting
  Approx 8"/15cm (22"/56cm in circumference)

yarn

Approx total: 445yd/407m wool medium
weight yarn

Color A: 245yd/224m in white

Color B: 200yd/183m in yellow

materials

Knitting needles: 6mm (size 10 U.S.) dpn
or size to obtain gauge

3.75mm (size 5 U.S.) needles for the band

Sewing needle and thread to match yarn color

Cotton crochet thread

Tapestry needle

Stitch marker

gauge before felting

15 sts and 21 rows = 4"/10cm with A in
Stockinette Stitch using larger needles
Always take time to check your gauge.

pattern stitches

Stockinette Stitch

Seed Stitch

INSTRUCTIONS

Using A and the larger needles, CO 5 sts on 4 dpn.
Join into a circle.

Rnd 1: K into front and back of ea st—10 sts.

Rnd 2: (Inc 1, k1) rep 5 times—15 sts.

Rnd 3: (Inc 1, k2) rep 5 times—20 sts.

Rnd 4: (Inc 1, k3) rep 5 times—25 sts.

Continue increasing 5 times in ea round until there

are 20 sts in ea section—100 sts total.

Work even in St st for 20 more rnds.

On the next rnd (k2tog, k8) 10 times—90 sts.

Work 10 rnds in St st.

Work the next 3 rnds as foll (for the brim):

(Inc 1, k8) 10 times—100 sts.

(Inc 1, k9) 10 times—110 sts.

(Inc 1, k10) 10 times—120 sts.

Work even for 10 rnds, BO, weave in ends.

felting

Cut a length of cotton thread to the head measurement plus 6"/15cm. Use the tapestry needle to weave the thread in and out of the hat along the rnd just before the last 3 increase rnds. Pull the cotton thread so you can tie it into a square knot 3"/8cm from ea end, making the hat the correct size. Try it on to check the size. Felt the hat in the washer, checking occasionally, until fully felted to the desired head size. Pull the hat into shape if necessary and let dry.

band

With B and smaller needles, CO 5 sts. Work in k1, p1 Seed st until piece fits around outside of hat (about 23"/58cm). Sew ends tog and slide onto hat.

this project was knit with

Harrisville Designs' *The Orchid Line*, 25% mohair/5% silk/70% fine wool, worsted weight, 3.5oz/100g = approx 245yd/225m per ball
(A) 1 ball, color White Orchid #226

Harrisville Designs' *New England Knitters Highland*, 100% virgin wool, worsted weight, 3.5oz/100g = approx 200yd/183m per ball
(B) 1 ball, color Marigold #67

multicolored mittens

Felted mittens are great—they'll keep the cold and snow out and improve with age. You'll

begin each mitten by casting on into the back loop of a crochet chain stitch; the advantage

of this technique is that you can pull the chain stitches out easily after the piece is felted,

then pick up the stitches from the cast-on row and work the cuffs.

finished measurements

before felting
　Approx 6¾ x 9½"/17 x 24cm (excluding the
　knitted cuffs)

after felting
　Approx 5¾ x 6½"/15 x 17cm (excluding the
　knitted cuffs—fits medium size hands)

yarn

Approx total: 344yd/315m wool medium weight yarn

materials

Knitting needles: 8mm (size 11 U.S.) *or size
to obtain gauge*

5.5mm (size 9 U.S.) dpn for the cuffs

Worsted weight cotton yarn

6mm (size H U.S.) crochet hook

Stitch holders

Stitch marker

gauge before felting

14 sts and 17 rows = 4"/10cm in Stockinette Stitch
using larger needles

Always take time to check your gauge.

pattern stitches

Stockinette Stitch

K2 P2 Rib Stitch

INSTRUCTIONS (make two)

With the crochet hook and cotton yarn, ch at least 32.

Using the wool yarn and larger needles, CO 32 sts
into the back loops of the cotton chain.

Row 1: K.

Row 2: P.

Row 3: Continuing in St st, inc 1 st ea end—34 sts.

Rows 4–18: Continue in St st, inc 1 st ea end every
3 rows—36, 38, 40, 42, 44 sts.

Rows 19–21: Work even.

thumbs

K just the 1st 6 sts, work even in St st for 7 rows.
Dec 1 st ea end on the next 2 RS rows—2 sts.
K2tog, BO, weave in end.

Attach a new length of yarn to the 6th st from the
other end of the knitting, and rep for the other side
of the thumb.

fingers

Work center section even in St st for 14 rows. Move
16 sts to st holder. Working the rem sts, dec 1 st at
ea end every RS row until there are 6 sts left. BO
rem sts. Rep for the 16 sts on the st holder.

assembly

Weave in loose ends.

Fold knitting in half lengthwise and sew the seam
along the side, thumb, and fingers.

felting

Felt in the washer, checking occasionally to make
sure that the mittens are felting evenly. When felted
to the correct size, adjust the mittens to the desired
shape and let them dry.

cuff

Remove the cotton ch, sliding dpn into the loops of
the mitten sts as you pull out the cotton yarn and
distribute the sts evenly over 3 or 4 dpn, pm.
Working in the round, k2, p2 rib for 6"/15cm or
desired length. BO, weave in ends.

this project was knit with

Reynolds Yarns' *Harmony*, 100% wool, worsted
weight, 4oz/113g = approx 172yd/157m per ball, 2
balls of color #3

green sweater jacket

This wonderful heathered yarn is part of what makes the felted section of this

sweater jacket so appealing. The knitted sleeves and ribbing add texture and detail.

Because the yarn felts so well, the neckline doesn't need any added finishing.

finished measurements of bodice

before felting
  Approx 24 (26, 29, 32, 35) x 26 (27, 29, 30, 31)"/
  61 (66, 74, 81, 89) x 66 (69, 74, 76, 79)cm

after felting
  Approx 17 (19, 21, 23, 25) x 19 (20, 21, 22, 23)"/
  43 (48, 53, 58, 64) x 48 (51, 53, 56, 58)cm (excluding
  ribbing added to bottom after felting)

measurements of finished garment

size	chest	bodice length	sleeve length
XS	34"/86cm	20"/51cm	22½"/57cm
S	38"/97cm	21"/53cm	23"/58cm
M	42"/107cm	22"/56cm	23"/58cm
L	46"/117cm	23"/58cm	24"/61cm
XL	50"/127cm	24"/61cm	25"/64cm

Note: Bodice length includes ribbing added
after felting, and sleeve length is 1"/3cm shorter
with cuffs rolled.

yarn

Approx total: 1200 (1200, 1400, 1400, 1600)yd/
1097 (1097, 1280, 1280, 1463)m wool worsted
weight yarn

materials

Knitting needles: 5.5mm (size 9 U.S.) 29"/74cm
circular or *size to obtain gauge*

3.5mm (size 4 U.S.) dpn

4mm (size 6 U.S.) 29"/74cm circular for ribbing

Worsted weight cotton yarn

Four 1–1½"/3–4cm buttons

Sewing needle

Thread to match yarn color

Tapestry needle

Stitch marker

gauge before felting

17 sts and 24 rows = 4"/10cm in Stockinette Stitch
using 5.5mm (size 9 U.S.) circular needle

Always take time to check your gauge.

pattern stitches

Stockinette Stitch

K1 P1 Rib Stitch

INSTRUCTIONS

bodice

Using the cotton yarn and the 5.5mm (size 9 U.S.)
circular needle, CO 200 (224, 247, 270, 294) sts. Join
into a circle, pm. K 1 rnd.

Change to the wool yarn and k 165 (174, 182, 191,
200) rnds or until piece measures 26 (27, 29, 30,
31)"/66 (69, 74, 76, 79)cm long, BO, weave in ends.

felting

Flatten the tube so that beg of the rnd is at the center front. Sew the top opening closed with wool
yarn. This will be the shoulder seam. Baste the bottom closed with cotton thread. Felt in the washer
until fully felted and 17 (19, 21, 23, 25) x 19 (20, 21,
22, 23)"/43 (48, 53, 58, 64) x 48 (51, 53, 56, 58)cm.
Remove the basting thread. Pull into a rectangular
shape if necessary and dry flat. Cut the center front,

tip

You can "adjust" the finished fit to
your measurements by cutting the
center front as needed. This will
change the number of stitches you
need to pick up for the ribbing.

neckline, and sleeve opening as shown in figure 1. To make sure the armholes are the same, cut one, then use it as a template for the other side.

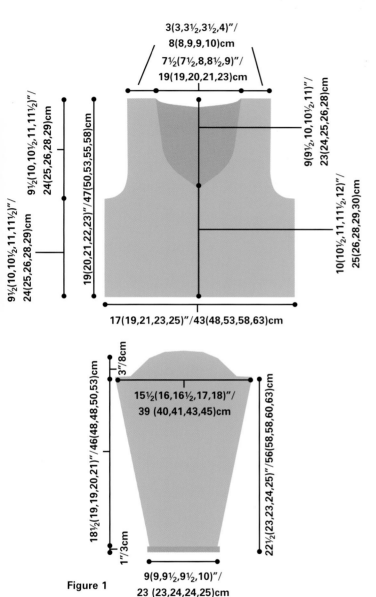

Figure 1

3(3,3½,3½,4)"/
8(8,9,9,10)cm

7½(7½,8,8½,9)"/
19(19,20,21,23)cm

9(9½,10,10½,11)"/
23(24,25,26,28)cm

9½(10,10½,11,11½)"/
24(25,26,28,29)cm

9½(10,10½,11,11½)"/
24(25,26,28,29)cm

19(20,21,22,23)"/47(50,53,55,58)cm

10(10½,11,11½,12)"/
25(26,28,29,30)cm

17(19,21,23,25)"/43(48,53,58,63)cm

3"/8cm

15½(16,16½,17,18)"/
39 (40,41,43,45)cm

18½(19,19,20,21)"/46(48,48,50,53)cm

1"/3cm

22½(23,23,24,25)"/56(58,58,60,63)cm

9(9,9½,9½,10)"/
23 (23,24,24,25)cm

ribbing

From WS, using the smaller 4mm (size 6 U.S.) circular needle, pick up the sts along the bottom edge by removing the cotton yarn as you pick up ea st. Work k1, p1 rib for 4 rows. BO. Weave in ends.

center front

Mark the position of the buttons.

Using dpn make about 12 (12, 12, 13, 14, 15)"/ 30 (30, 30, 33, 36, 38)cm of 3-stitch I-cord. Using matching sewing thread, sew the I-cord to the edge of the center front, leaving a loop large enough for each button. Unravel any extra length of I-cord to the top of the center front, BO, then weave in the end.

sleeve (make two)

Using larger 5.5mm (size 9 U.S.) circular, CO 38 (38, 40, 40, 42) sts. Work in St st throughout.

Work 12 rows even.

Inc 1 st ea side every 6th row 14 (15, 15, 16, 17) times—66 (68, 70, 72, 76) sts.

Work even for 20 rows.

BO 6 (6, 6, 7, 8) sts at beg of next two rows—54 (56, 58, 58, 60) sts.

Dec 1 st at ea end every other row 6 times—42 (44, 46, 46, 48) sts.

Dec 1 st at ea end every row 4 times—34 (36, 38, 38, 40) sts.

BO. Weave in ends.

Steam-press sleeve except for cuff.

assembly

Sew the buttons across from the loops you made with the I-cord. Sew the sleeve seams tog with yarn. Pin the sleeves ¼"/6mm on the inside of the bodice, matching center tops and bottoms. Working from the inside, sew the sleeve to the bodice with matching sewing thread.

this project was knit in size extra small with

Harrisville Designs' *New England Knitters Highland*, 100% virgin wool, worsted weight, 3.5oz/100g = approx 200yd/183m per ball, 6 balls of color Seagreen #12

experience level

intermediate

This easy-to-make project is an improvement over the standard mesh market bag since the firm felted bottom keeps items safe. The trickiest part of the construction is picking up the stitches along the finished bottom when you get ready to knit the sides. Solve this by using smaller needles at first, then working up to larger needles.

finished
measurements of felted bottom

before felting
  Approx 17½"/45cm diameter

after felting
  Approx 12"/30cm diameter

yarn

Approx total: 440yd/402m wool medium weight yarn

Color A: 220yd/201m in turquoise

Color B: 220yd/201m in blue

materials

Knitting needles: 4.5mm (size 7 U.S.) dpn and 20"/51cm circular or *size to obtain gauge*

Stitch marker

4mm (size G U.S.) crochet hook

Worsted weight cotton yarn

Tapestry needle

4mm (size 6 U.S.) 20"/51cm circular

8mm (size 11 U.S.) 20"/51cm circular

gauge before felting

19 sts and 24 rows = 4"/10cm in Stockinette Stitch using 4.5mm (size 7 U.S.) needles

Always take time to check your gauge.

stitch pattern

Stockinette Stitch

INSTRUCTIONS
bag bottom

Using A and 4.5mm (size 7 U.S) dpn, CO 5 sts. Join into a circle, pm.

Rnd 1: K into front and back of ea st—10 sts.

Rnd 2: (Inc 1, k1) rep 5 times—15 sts.

Rnd 3: (Inc 1, k2) rep 5 times—20 sts.

Rnd 4: (Inc 1, k3) rep 5 times—25 sts.

Continue increasing 5 times in ea rnd until there are 32 sts in ea section—160 sts total.

Work even in St st for 20 more rnds.

Change to cotton yarn. Work 1 rnd. Use crochet hook to BO in sc. Cut yarn to 3"/8cm, pass through last loop. Do not weave in end of cotton yarn. You'll need to get to it easily to take out the cotton yarn after felting. Weave in all ends of wool yarn.

felting

Felt in the washer as desired. Let dry.

bag sides

Pull out cotton yarn, picking up all sts with B and smallest circular needle, pm—160 sts.

Change to the next-largest size circular needle and k 1 rnd.

Change to the largest size circular needle and k2tog, rep around—80 sts.

Work next rnd with (k2tog, yo).

Rep last rnd 33 times or until bag is desired length.

Change to smallest circular needle (k into front and back, k1) around.

K 3 rnds even.

BO with crochet hook in sc.

Change to A and work 1 rnd of sc. Weave in ends.

handles (make two)

Make 4-stitch I-cord with dpn and 2 strands of A held tog as 1, 41 rnds. Sew handle to top edge of bag, about 2½"/6cm from either side of center front. Rep for other handle, attaching 2½"/6cm from either side of center back. Weave in ends.

this project was knit with

Cascade Yarn's *Cascade 220*, 100% Peruvian Highland wool, worsted weight, 3.5oz/100g = approx 220yd/201m per ball

(A) 1 ball, color Turquoise #7919

(B) 1 ball, color Blue #7818

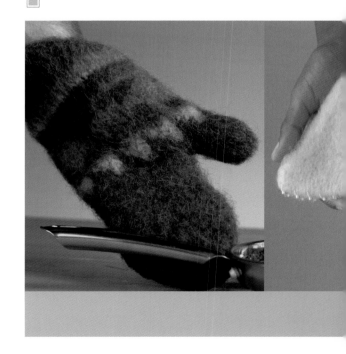

embroidery

Embroidery is a wonderful companion to felted knits, whether you chose to embroider before or after you felt your project. Because the felting fuzzes up all the colors of yarn, you can correct color design errors that happened in the knitting stage. Or you can add a touch of color you didn't think you needed while you were knitting; it will blend in perfectly during the felting process. You could also work a duplicate stitch design. This technique is great if you prefer embroidery to colorwork but want to have a color design in your project just the same. It's a breeze to anchor beads, floss, or yarn across the stable fuzzy surface, and hiding thread ends in the felted surface couldn't be easier.

This project is a great example of the versatility of felting. By basting the top opening of the purse before felting, the rest of the clutch gently stretches toward its corners. Then you hand felt the flap, cut it in a gentle arc, and embellish it with beads.

finished measurements

before felting (basted, ready to felt)
  Approx 12 x 7"/30 x 18cm
after felting
  Approx 13 x 4¾"/33 x 12cm

yarn

Approx total: 327yd/300m wool fine weight yarn

Materials

Knitting needles: 5.5mm (size 9 U.S.)
or size to obtain gauge

Cotton crochet thread

Tapestry needle

Fabric scissors

Beads (see figure 1)

Beading needle and beading thread to match yarn color

gauge before felting

17 sts and 21 rows = 4"/10cm in Stockinette Stitch

Always take time to check your gauge.

pattern stitch

Stockinette Stitch

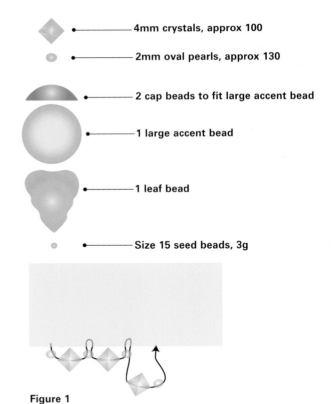

4mm crystals, approx 100

2mm oval pearls, approx 130

2 cap beads to fit large accent bead

1 large accent bead

1 leaf bead

Size 15 seed beads, 3g

Figure 1

INSTRUCTIONS

CO 50 sts. Work in St st for 90 rows or until piece measures 18"/46cm long, BO, weave in ends.

felting

Fold the bottom up 6"/15cm, then sew the sides with the wool yarn. Using the cotton crochet thread, baste the opening to the bag. Fold the top flap in half as shown in figure 2 and baste in place with the cotton crochet thread. Felt in the washer. The finished piece will have an hourglass shape. Take out the basting stitches and continue to hand-felt the flap as desired. Let it dry. Cut the flap into a wide arc that's 3¼"/8cm deep at the center.

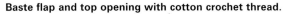

Baste flap and top opening with cotton crochet thread.

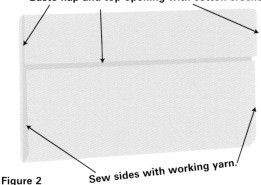

Figure 2

Sew sides with working yarn.

bead embroidery

Following the illustrations in figure 1, stitch the beads to the edge of the flap. Knot the beading thread and weave in the ends. Attach a new thread at the center front of the flap and add the large accent beads as shown in figure 3.

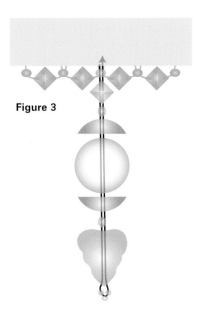

Figure 3

Attach a new length of thread at one bottom corner of the bag and sew the loops of beads along the bottom edge as shown in figure 4.

Figure 4

this project was knit with

Dale of Norway's *Heilo*, 100% pure wool, sport weight, 1.75oz/50g = approx 109yd/100m per ball, 3 balls of color Peach #3102

experience level

easy ●

A great pattern for felting, this easy-to-make hat works up in an afternoon. It's a perfect example of the flaring effect that happens when you felt knitwear in the washing machine. The embroidery adds detail and helps shape the brim.

finished measurements

before felting

Approx 15 x 13"/38 x 33cm

after felting

Approx 14 x 8"/36 x 20cm (to fit head measuring 22"/56cm in circumference)

yarn

Approx total: 1200yd/1098m wool worsted weight yarn

Color A: 200yd/183m in teal blue

Color B: 200yd/183m in green

Color C: 200yd/183m in yellow green

Color D: 200yd/183m in forest green

Color E: 200yd/183m in magenta

Color F: 200yd/183m in violet

materials

Knitting needles: 5.5mm (size 9 U.S.) 24"/61cm circular *or size to obtain gauge*

Tapestry needle

gauge before felting

16 sts and 20 rows = 4"/10cm in Stockinette Stitch

Always take time to check your gauge.

pattern stitch

Stockinette Stitch

INSTRUCTIONS

With A, CO 108 sts. Join into a circle, being careful not to twist the stitches.

Work 12 rnds in A, 4 rnds in C, 28 rnds in B, 4 rnds in C, and 12 rnds in A.

Work decreases for crown of hat as foll:

Rnd 1: (K16, k2tog) rep 6 times—102 sts.

Rnd 2 and all even rnds: K.

Rnd 3: (K15, k2tog) rep 6 times—96 sts.

Rnd 5: (K14, k2tog) rep 6 times—90 sts.

Continue decreasing 6 times every other rnd until you have 12 sts left. Cut yarn to 8"/20cm and pass through rem sts. Weave in end.

embroidery

Using wool yarn and following figure 1, chain stitch the stem. Use stem stitch for the curling vines and straight stitch for the flowers and leaves.

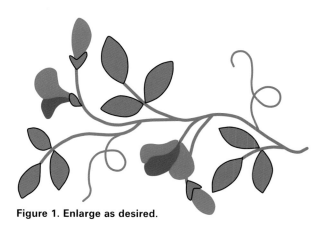

Figure 1. Enlarge as desired.

felting

Felt in the washer, checking to see if the brim is flaring out too much. If it is, especially below the embroidery, use A to stitch along the inside of the brim and gather it slightly to pull it back into shape. Continue felting. Try on the hat and shape it to your head, then let it dry.

this project was knit with

Harrisville Designs' *New England Knitters Highland*, 100% virgin wool, worsted weight, 3.5oz/100g = approx 200yd/183m per ball

(A) 1 ball, color Teal Blue #16

(B) 1 ball, color Seagreen #12

(C) 1 ball, color Tundra #7

(D) 1 ball, color Cypress #69

(E) 1 ball, color Magenta #23

(F) 1 ball, color Violet #21

pink embroidered scarf

Have leftover felting yarn? By working two strands of yarn together as one and switching one yarn periodically you will create an interesting pattern, changing the color and texture. An embroidery pattern as simple as a swirling line can add a special touch.

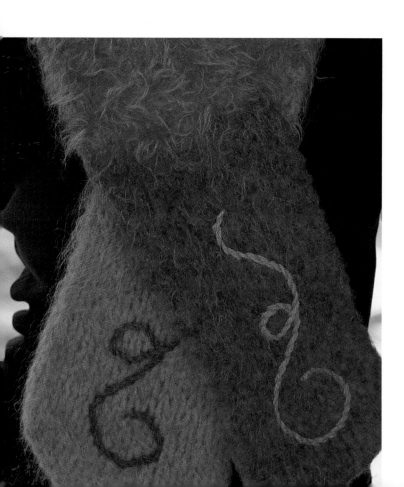

finished measurements

before felting
   Approx 8 x 49"/20 x 124cm

after felting
   Approx 6 x 52"/15 x 132cm

yarn

Approx total: 477yd/436m wool or wool blend worsted weight yarn

Color A: 55yd/50m of bulky weight yarn, wool, in pink

Color B: 90yd/82m of worsted weight yarn, mohair/wool/nylon blend, in pink

Color C: 94yd/86m of heavy worsted weight yarn, wool/viscose/nylon blend, in dark pink

Color D: 109yd/100m of light worsted weight yarn, alpaca, in maroon

Color E: 129yd/118m of light worsted weight yarn, alpaca/silk/wool blend, in pink

materials

Knitting needles: 15mm (size 19 U.S.) *or size to obtain gauge*

Cotton crochet thread

Tapestry needle

gauge before felting

7 sts and 10 rows = 4"/10cm in Stockinette Stitch

Always take time to check your gauge.

pattern stitch

Stockinette Stitch

INSTRUCTIONS

Using A and B held tog as one, CO 14 sts. Work in St st throughout.

Work 27 rows.

Change to B and C and work 58 rows.

Change to C and D and work 32 rows, BO, weave in ends.

felting

Fold in half and baste sides tog with cotton crochet thread. Felt in the washer. Take out the cotton crochet thread while the scarf is still wet and pull the scarf out as long as possible, shaping the ends into a curve and straightening the sides. Let dry.

embroidery

With the tapestry needle, use stem stitch to embroider the dark end of the scarf with E and embroider the light end of the scarf with D. Use the design template on page 123 if desired.

this project was knit with

Classic Elite Yarns' *Two.Two*, 100% Highland wool, bulky weight, 1.75oz/50g = approx 55yd/50m per ball

(A) 1 ball, color #1532

Classic Elite Yarns' *La Gran*, 76.5% mohair/17.5% wool/6% nylon, worsted weight, 1.5oz/42g = approx 90yd/82m per ball

(B) 1 ball, color #6589

Classic Elite Yarns' *Gatsby*, 70% wool/15% viscose/15% nylon, heavy worsted weight, 3.5oz/100g = approx 94yd/86m per ball

(C) 1 ball, color #2132

Classic Elite Yarns' *Inca Alpaca*, 100% alpaca, light worsted weight, 1.75oz/50g = approx 109yd/100m per ball

(D) 1 ball, color #1142

Classic Elite Yarns' *Wings*, 50% alpaca/23% silk/22% wool, light worsted weight, 1.75oz/50g = approx 129yd/118m per ball

(E) 1 ball, color #2332

tip

This project would be a great way to experiment with combining yarn if you want make something other than a basic swatch.

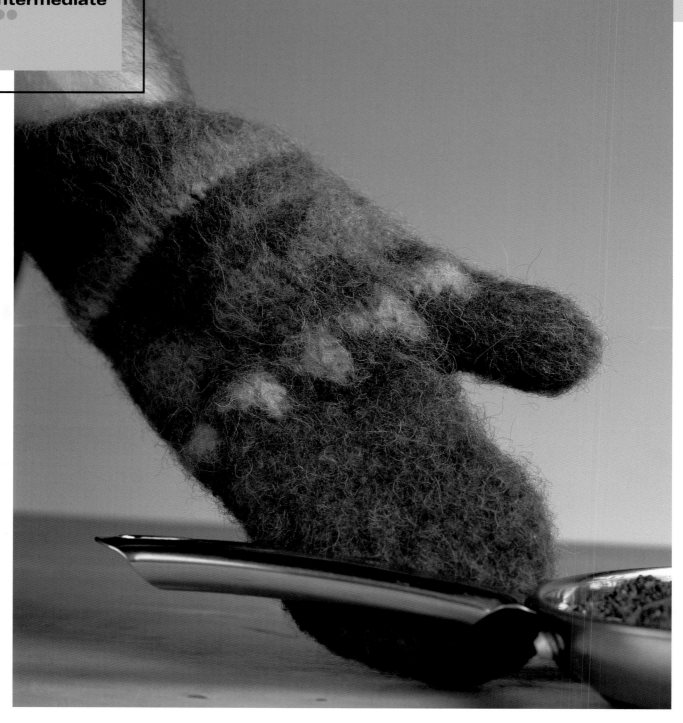

This handy (and thick!) oven mitt is worked flat, then embroidered in duplicate stitch before being assembled. Because it's extra long, this mitt will protect your arm.

finished measurements

before felting
   Approx 7 x 20"/18 x 51cm, not including I-cord loop

after felting
   Approx 6 x 15"/15 x 38cm, not including I-cord loop

yarn

Approx total: 330yd/303m wool bulky weight yarn

Color A: 110yd/101m in blue

Color B: 110yd/101m in green

Color C: 110yd/101m in yellow

materials

Knitting needles: 8mm (size 11 U.S.) *or size to obtain gauge*

8mm (size 11 U.S.) dpn for the I-cord

Cotton crochet thread

Tapestry needle

3 stitch holders

gauge before felting

11 sts and 15 rows = 4"/10cm in Stockinette Stitch

Always take time to check your gauge.

pattern stitch

Stockinette Stitch

INSTRUCTIONS

i-cord loop

Using the dpn and A, begin with a 12"/31cm tail and CO 3 sts.

Rnd 1–Rnd 20: Work 3-stitch I-cord.

arm and wrist section

Rows 21–38: Beg with a P row, inc 1 st at beg and end of ea row, working in St st—39 sts after row 38.

Rows 39–57: Work even.

Row 58: Inc 1 st ea end—41 sts.

Rows 59–61: Work even.

Rows 62–65: Rep rows 58–61—43 sts.

Row 66: Rep row 58—45 sts.

palm and fingers section

Row 67: P 1st 7 sts, move to st holder, p to last 7 sts, move last 7 sts to st holder.

Work 17 rows even—31 sts.

K 1st 15 sts, then move them to st holder, BO center st.

Working one side of mitt, dec 1 st ea end on every RS row until there are 5 sts left. BO. Attach new length of yarn and rep for 15 sts on st holder.

thumbs

Working one of the 7 sts on the holder and beg on the right side, attach a new length of yarn and work 7 rows even in St st.

Dec 1 st ea end on the next 2 RS rows—3 sts.

On the next row k3tog, BO.

Rep for the other 7 sts on holder to make the other side of the thumb.

embroidery

Following the chart in figure 1, embroider the yellow and green pattern by duplicate stitching over the knit stitches, covering one stitch for each square in the chart. Rep the pattern in reverse, if desired, for the other side of the mitt.

assembly

Weave in any loose strands of yarn from the embroidery. Sew the I-cord section into a loop using the 12"/31cm tail at the beg of the knitting. Fold knitting in half lengthwise and sew the seam along the side, thumb, and fingers.

felting

Using the cotton crochet thread, baste the bottom opening of the mitt closed.

Felt in the washer, checking occasionally to make sure that the mitt is felting evenly. When fully felted, remove the cotton crochet thread from the bottom opening. Adjust the mitt to the desired finished shape and let dry.

this project was knit with

Reynolds Yarns' *Lopi*, 100% virgin wool, bulky weight, 3.5oz/100g =approx 110yd/100m per skein

(A) 1 skein, color Blue #735

(B) 1 skein, color Grass Green #212

(C) 1 ball, Yellow #213

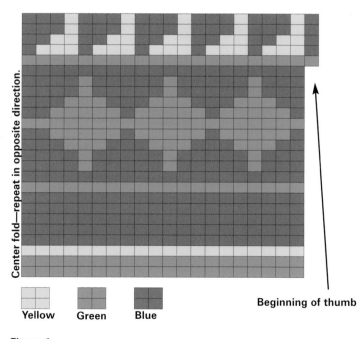

Center fold—repeat in opposite direction.

Beginning of thumb

Yellow   Green   Blue

Figure 1

The duplicate stitch embroidery makes this project special. The little decorative

ball is an added feature that's fun and easy to make.

finished measurements

before felting

Individual Section: Approx 6½ x 7½"/17 x 19cm

after felting

Individual Section: Approx 6 x 6½"/15 x 17cm

Finished Tam: Approx 11"/28cm across top (to fit head measuring 22"/56cm in circumference)

yarn

Approx total: 436yd/399m wool worsted weight yarn

Color A: 218yd/199m in gray

Color B: 109yd/100m in purple

Color C: 109yd/100m in white

materials

Knitting needles: 4.5mm (size 7 U.S.) *or size to obtain gauge*

3.75mm (size 5 U.S.) dpn

Fabric scissors

5 stitch holders

Cotton crochet thread

Tapestry needle

Stitch marker

11"/28cm plate

gauge before felting

18 ½ sts and 24 rows = 4"/10cm in Stockinette Stitch using larger needles

Always take time to check your gauge.

pattern stitches

Stockinette Stitch

K2 P2 Rib Stitch

INSTRUCTIONS

hat section (make five)

Using the larger needles and A, CO 1 st.

Row 1: K into the front and back of the st—2 sts.

Row 2: P into the front and back of the st, k1—3 sts.

Row 3: K into the front and back of the 1st st, k rem sts—4 sts.

Row 4: P into front and back of 1st st, p rem sts—5 sts.

Rep rows 3 and 4 until you have 30 sts. Work even for 8 more rows.

Continuing in St st, on the next 3 RS rows, dec 1 st at the beg and end of the row—28, 26, 24 sts.

P the last row, move sts to st holder.

Sew sections tog along sides with A.

Follow chart in figure 1 for duplicate stitch.

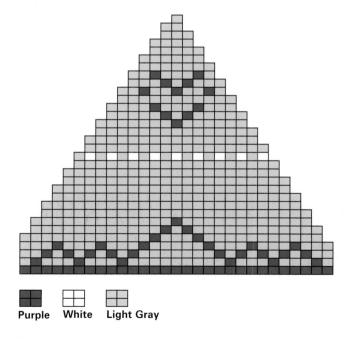

■	⊞	☐
Purple	**White**	**Light Gray**

Figure 1

felting

Thread cotton crochet thread through all sts on holders, pull thread to 21"/53cm and tie in a knot. Felt in washer until the desired size. Let dry.

assembly

Untie the knot in the cotton thread and pick up all sts around on 3.75mm (size 5 U.S.) dpn, pm—120 sts. Work in k2, p2 rib for 2½"/6cm, BO loosely in pat. Weave in ends.

Wet tam and pull over the plate so end of embroidery pat is at edge of the plate. Let dry and remove plate.

ball

Using B and size 4.5mm (size 7 U.S.) needles, CO 5 sts, work in St st for 8 rows. Cut yarn to 8"/20cm and weave through all rem sts. Weave in along sides and CO edge. Hand felt. Sew to center top of tam.

this project was knit with

Reynolds Yarns' *Lite-Lopi*, 100% virgin wool, worsted weight, 1.75oz/50g = approx 109yd/100m per ball

(A) 2 balls, color Light Gray #56

(B) 1 ball, color Purple #440

(C) 1 ball, color White #51

cut & sew

Now we'll explore an area of felted knits that hasn't received much attention. Once a piece of knitting is felted, it really has become something different—it's now a piece of fabric. Unlike the original knitted item that quickly unravels when cut and stretches awkwardly under the sewing machine needle, felted knitting makes a nice thick fabric that's ready to sew, similar to acrylic fleece.

Of course, this property is only present in a fully felted knit. If just the surface is felted the fabric will begin to fray when you cut it, unraveling stitch by stitch. So the projects in this section need to be felted as thoroughly as possible before you begin sewing, as they'll have exposed raw edges. Felting the projects well doesn't mean that you won't see the stitches a little bit when you cut into the felted fabric, but they won't start to fall apart at the edges.

These cut-and-sew projects lend themselves beautifully to details, from embroidery to Mola-style reverse appliqué. Because the felted fabric is so thick, it's a great protective layer for a lined knitting needle case. Three-dimensional projects with cutouts (like a pair of fingerless gloves) are perfect for this technique. Pillows are a cinch since you don't have to worry about finishing the raw edges. Making a lined purse is easier than you might think—no finishing the raw edges there either—and the felt holds its shape very well. An added bonus is that you can choose which side of the felted knitting to use in your project; one may offer you a more interesting texture. The knitting is easy for all of the projects in this section, but you also need to be comfortable using a sewing machine.

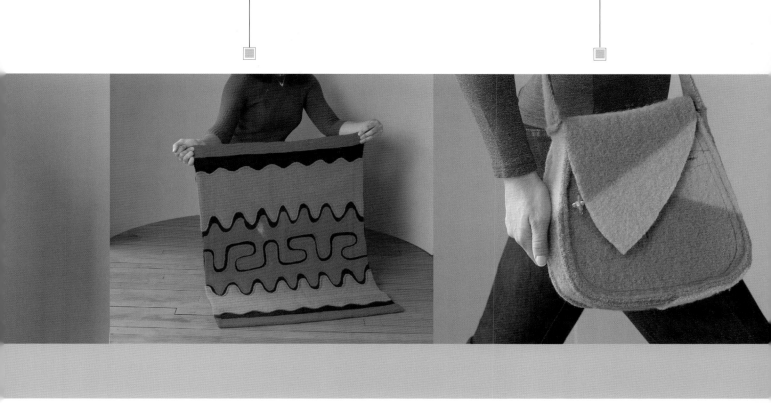

mola-style rug

Molas made with delicate reverse appliqué were traditionally used for the bodice sections of blouses made by the Kuna women of Panama. This project mimics the mola technique in a couple of ways: you stitch through layers of fabric and cut to expose a different color below, and you use bright colors to create a bold, geometric design.

finished measurements

before felting
Four rectangles: each approx 20 x 32"/
51 x 81cm
after felting
Four rectangles: each approx 17 x 24"/43 x
61cm, to be sewn into a 24 x 33"/61 x 84cm rug

yarn

Approx total: 1760yd/1608m wool medium weight yarn

Color A: 440yd/402m in red

Color B: 440yd/402m in orange

Color C: 440yd/402m in green

Color D: 440yd/402m in purple

materials

Knitting needles: 5.5mm (size 9 U.S.) *or size to obtain gauge*

Sewing machine and thread to match colors A and B

Cotton crochet thread

Tapestry needle

Fabric scissors

1yd/1m of backing fabric (optional)

gauge before felting

18 sts and 24 rows = 4"/10cm in Stockinette Stitch
Always take time to check your gauge.

stitch pattern

Stockinette Stitch

INSTRUCTIONS

With A, CO 90 sts. Work in St st for 32"/81cm, BO, weave in ends.
Rep with B, C, and D.

felting

Baste A and B tog, one atop the other, with the cotton crochet thread. Baste C and D tog also. Felt in the washer until fully felted to 17 x 24"/43 x 61cm rectangles. (I felted the orange and red separately from the green and purple so the colors wouldn't mix.) Remove the cotton crochet thread and pull the pieces into equal-sized rectangles if necessary. Dry flat.

assembly

Cut A into two 3 x 24"/8 x 61cm strips and one 11 x 24"/28 x 61cm strip.

Cut B into two 8 ½ x 24"/22 x 61cm strips.

Cut C into two 5 x 24"/13 x 61cm strips and one 7 x 24"/18 x 61cm strip.

Cut D into two 8 ½ x 24"/22cm x 61cm strips.

On the 11"/28cm wide strip in color A, use a pen to draw the center pattern and the wavy sides as shown. (Use the templates on pages 124 and 125 if desired.) Center the 7"/18cm wide strip in color C underneath the 11"/28cm wide strip in A and pin. Using thread that matches color A, stitch about ¼–½"/6–13mm away from the pattern (figure 1). Rep on the other side of the line. Cut A close to the stitching lines so C is showing.

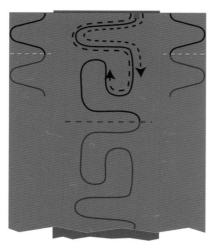

Figure 1. Flip center pattern to repeat.

Pin each D strip under the sewn A strip so they extend past the wavy lines by about 1"/3cm. Cut away any part of the sewn C strip that is overlapping the D strip. Stitch about ¼–½"/6–13mm away from the wavy line and cut A close to the stitching as shown (figure 2). Rep for the other side.

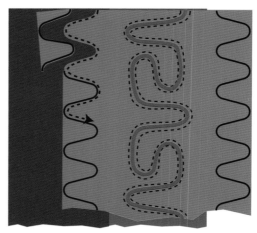

Figure 2

Pin one B piece on top of the sewn piece so that it slightly overlaps one of the wavy lines of stitching. Pin the other B piece over the other wavy line. Turn the rug over and stitch from the back side about ¾–1"/2–3cm away from the wavy line of stitching (figure 3). Turn right side up and cut the B pieces close to the stitching, so that D shows between A and B.

Figure 3

Pin the rem strips of C at each end, under B, so they extend beyond the sewn pieces and sew a shallow wavy line on B. Cut close to the stitching so C shows (figure 4).

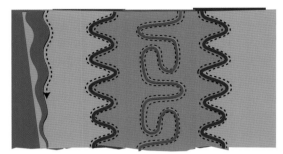

Figure 4

Pin the two rem strips of A over C at both ends of the rug, overlapping C about 1"/3cm. Stitch close to the edge of A and trim if necessary. Fold A under about ¾"/2cm and top-stitch two rows about ¼"/6mm apart.

finishing (optional)

Use flannel or other material as a backing to cover the raw edges of C and D.

this project was knit with

Cascade Yarns' *Cascade 220*, 100% Peruvian Highland wool, worsted weight, 3.5oz/100g = approx 220yd/201m per ball
(A) 2 balls, color Red #8414
(B) 2 balls, color Burnt Orange #7824
(C) 2 balls, color Hunter Green #8893
(D) 2 balls, color Italian Plum #8886

note

The word "mola" means "blouse" in the Kuna language. Molas are unique because the intricate designs are cut through many layers of fabric to expose the contrasting colors below. The women spend a great deal of time turning under the raw edges of the upper layers to finish the designs. Although this project is similar to a mola, it is a relatively simple interpretation of the technique because the felted knitting is too thick to work with more than two layers. There are also no worries about raw edges, since they are felted and don't fray!

experience level

knitting ●
easy

sewing ●
easy

This easy-to-knit needle case will become an indispensable item in your knitting bag. Tailor it to your personality by choosing a lining fabric that displays your inner self, be it bright and sunny or mellow and calm.

finished measurements

before felting
   Approx 17 x 32"/43 x 81cm

after felting
   Approx 14½ x 19"/37 x 48cm

yarn

Approx total: 110yd/100m wool bulky weight yarn

materials

Knitting needles: 8mm (size 11 U.S.) *or size to obtain gauge*

Fabric scissors

13 x 19½"/33 x 50cm piece of fabric for lining

20 x 19½"/51 x 50cm piece of fabric for pockets

6 x 19½"/15 x 50cm piece of fabric for flap

Cotton crochet thread

Tapestry needle

Sewing needle and thread to match fabric color and yarn colors

Sewing machine

24"/61cm of ribbon, 1¼"/3cm wide

gauge before felting

11½ sts and 15 rows = 4"/10cm in Stockinette Stitch

Always take time to check your gauge.

INSTRUCTIONS

CO 50 sts. Work in St st for 117 rows, or until piece measures 32"/81cm long. BO, weave in ends.

felting

Fold in half and baste all edges tog with cotton crochet thread. Felt in the washer until fully felted. Remove the basting and adjust to an even rectangle. Let dry flat.

assembly

Fold one long side of the lining fabric under ½"/13mm and press. Fold the pocket fabric in half so it's 10½ x 19½"/27 x 50cm and press. Place the pocket piece over the lining piece and stitch dividers as shown (figure 1). Fold the raw edges under ½"/13mm and press. Edgestitch to the felted piece. Fold the flap piece in half lengthwise, RS tog. Stitch ¼"/6mm from the raw edges, leaving a 3"/8cm opening. Trim the corners, turn RS out, and press. Hand sew the opening closed. Stitch the flap to the top edge of the felting. Sew the center of the ribbon to the outside center edge of the felted piece, matching the line of stitching.

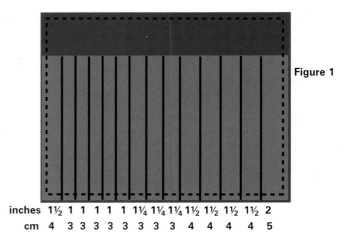

Figure 1

inches	1½	1	1	1	1	1	1¼	1¼	1¼	1½	1½	1½	1½	2
cm	4	3	3	3	3	3	3	3	3	4	4	4	4	5

this project was knit with

Classic Elite Yarns' *Paintbox*, 100% merino wool, chunky weight, 1.75oz/50g = approx 55yd/50m per ball, 2 balls of color Cerulean Blue #6820

fingerless gloves

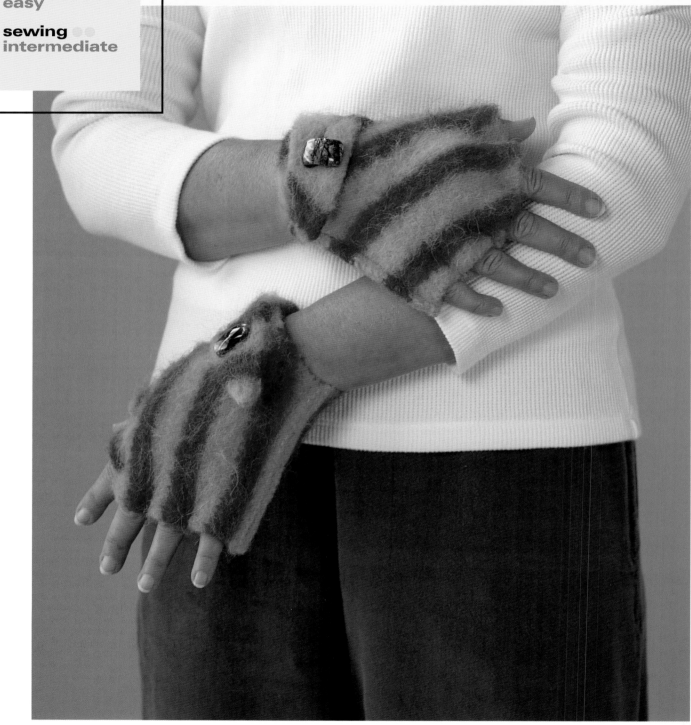

Gloves have never been this easy. After you've felted your knitted rectangles, just cut, sew, and you've got it!

finished measurements

before felting
Fabric: Approx 7 x 6½"/18 x 17cm

after felting
Gloves: Approx 3"/8cm across the palm (fits medium size hand)

yarn

Approx total: 436yd/400m wool DK weight yarn
Color A: 218yd/200m in yellow
Color B: 109yd/100m in red
Color C: 109yd/100m in purple

materials

Knitting needles: 5.5mm (size 9 U.S.) *or size to obtain gauge*
Tapestry needle
Fabric scissors
Sewing machine
Iron
Two ¾–1½"/ 2–4cm decorative buttons
Sewing needle and thread to match yarn color

gauge before felting

16 sts and 20 rows = 4"/10cm in Stockinette Stitch
Always take time to check your gauge.

pattern stitch

Stockinette Stitch

INSTRUCTIONS (make two)

CO 40 sts in A. Work 8 rows. Rep the foll color pat 9 times:
2 rows of B, 2 rows of C, 2 rows of B, 8 rows of A.
BO. Weave in ends. Fold in half lengthwise and sew all edges tog with color A, so you have a rectangle.

felting

Felt in the washer until fully felted. Pull each piece into a rectangle or square that's at least 9"/23cm each way. Do not cut open. Let dry.

assembly

Each glove has a front and a back piece; the back piece will have the button flap. You'll begin by cutting these pieces out at the same time, but you'll finish cutting each separately because you need to use the fabric around the fold to cut out the flap.

Copy the template from page 125. Arrange it on one of the felted rectangles with the stripes in the direction you choose. Pin in place. Cut through both layers along the little finger side, the bottom, and the finger openings. Now, *cutting through one layer only*, cut along the thumb side of the front (the dotted line on the template.) Finish cutting the back (with the button flap) using the fabric left over from cutting the front.

Machine sew the little finger side and then the thumb side to the beginning of the button flap, using a 1/4"/6mm or smaller seam allowance. Sew the finger and thumb divisions as shown on the template. Try the glove on to make sure it fits. If any of the finger openings are too small, rip out the lines of stitching and sew again. Try it once more. When it fits to your satisfaction, take it off and cut between the finger and thumb stitching.

Steam the glove with the iron and let it cool enough to put on. Then mold it to your hand, firmly pulling the button flap into place and holding it there until the glove has cooled down.

Sew the button on at the center, about 1"/3cm from the bottom edge of the glove. Try on the glove and mark the position of the buttonhole on the flap. Cut the buttonhole and trim the point of the flap, if necessary, so it's not too long. Brush and hand felt the edges of the glove if desired.

Repeat for the other glove, reversing the template so that the button flap will come around from the other side of the glove to fit the other hand.

this project was knit with

Reynolds Yarns' *Lite-Lopi*, 100% virgin wool, worsted weight, 1.75oz/50g = approx 109yd/100m per ball

(A) 2 ball, color yellow #435

(B) 1 balls, color red #434

(C) 1 ball, color purple #440

tip

If you're not sure how your gloves will come out, try it first with doubled 9 x 12"/23 x 30cm sheets of synthetic felt. You'll then have created the perfect pattern for your felted knitting project.

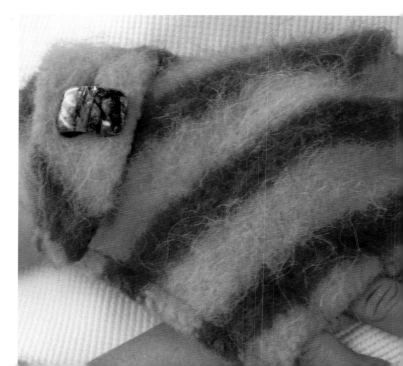

perfect floor pillow

The fun part of this project is cutting the undulating line across the felting. I made this one big with a simple design, but you could just as easily make a small throw pillow following a machine appliqué pattern or a quilting block design. Just about any simple motif will work.

finished measurements

before felting

  Purple rectangle: Approx 25 x 24"/64 x 61cm
  Blue rectangle: Approx 17½ x 44"/44 x 112cm

after felting

  Purple rectangle: Approx 20 x 18"/51 x 46cm
  Blue rectangle: Approx 14 x 34"/36 x 86cm
  Rectangles combine to make a 24"/61cm pillow.

yarn

Approx total: 1050yd/966m lightweight wool yarn

Color A: 525yd/483m in lavender

Color B: 525yd/483m in light blue

materials

Knitting needles: 4.5mm (size 7 U.S.) *or size to obtain gauge*

Cotton crochet thread

Fabric scissors

Tapestry needle

25"/64cm square of backing fabric

24"/61cm square pillow form

Sewing needle and thread to match backing fabric and colors A and B

Sewing machine

gauge before felting

16 sts and 22 rows = 4"/10cm in Stockinette Stitch

Always take time to check your gauge.

pattern stitch

Stockinette Stitch

INSTRUCTIONS

purple rectangle

CO 100 sts. Work in St st for 131 rows or until piece measures 24"/61cm. BO. Weave in ends.

blue rectangle

CO 70 sts. Work in St st for 246 rows or until piece measures 44"/112cm. BO. Weave in ends.

felting

Fold each rectangle in half and sew the sides together loosely with the tapestry needle and cotton crochet thread. Felt in the washer until the knitting is fully felted. Remove the cotton thread. Adjust if necessary into 20 x 18"/51 x 46 (A) and 14 x 34"/36 x 86cm (B) rectangles. Let both dry.

assembly

Cut the A rectangle in half from one corner to the other along a wavy diagonal line. Place the A pieces on the B rectangle, arranging them to create a 24"/61cm square. It's easiest to line the first A section up on a table, then slide the B rectangle under it and adjust the other A section until you have 24"/61cm in length and width. Pin in place along the wavy edge of the A sections. Topstitch on the A sections, through both layers of felting, ⅛"/3mm to ¼"/6mm from the edge. Turn the piece over and cut B about ⅛"/3mm to ¼"/6mm from the stitching line.

Turn all the edges of the backing fabric under ½"/13mm and press. Pin the backing fabric to the wrong side of the felted piece all along the edges, letting the felt piece overlap the backing slightly so the backing won't show when the pieces are stitched together. Machine stitching about ⅛"/3mm from the folded edge, sew the backing to the felted piece, leaving enough of an opening in one side to

insert the pillow form. Topstitch along the opening through the felted layer *only* so the finished front will have a continuous stitching line.

Squeeze the pillow form into the pillow, taking time to make sure the corners of the form fill the corners of the pillow. Stitch the opening closed with the needle and thread.

this project was knit with

Baabajoes' *Wool Pak*, 8-ply, 100% pure new wool, light worsted weight, 8.75oz/250g = approx 525yd/483m per ball

(A) 1 ball, color Periwinkle #32

(B) 1 ball, color Bluebell #33

experience level

knitting
easy ●

sewing
advanced ●●●

finished measurements

before felting
  Rectangle: Approx 23 x 60"/58 x 152cm
after felting
  Rectangle: Approx 18 x 42"/46 x 107cm
  Purse: Approx 10 x 10"/25 x 25cm

yarn

Approx total: 872yd/800m wool fine weight yarn
Color A: 218yd/200m in gray
Color B: 218yd/200m in brass
Color C: 218yd/200m in gold
Color D: 218yd/200m in brown

materials

Knitting needles: 5mm (size 8 U.S.)
or size to obtain gauge
Cotton crochet thread
Tapestry needle
Graph paper and pencil
Craft scissors and fabric scissors
1yd/1m lining fabric
Sewing needle and thread to match yarn color
Sewing machine

gauge before felting

17 sts and 24 rows = 4"/10cm in Stockinette Stitch
Always take time to check your gauge.

pattern stitch

Stockinette Stitch

Here's a project that truly combines knitting, felting, and sewing, so you can use all your skills. It's easier than making the same purse with fabric since you don't have to turn under your raw edges. The thick felted knitting makes this bag nice and sturdy.

INSTRUCTIONS

strap

CO 10 sts in B, work 220 rows in St st, BO, weave in ends.

large rectangle for purse fabric

CO 100 sts in A, working in St st throughout, finish all A, change to B, work all B, change to C, work all C, change to D, work all D, BO, weave in ends.

felting

Fold the strap in half lengthwise; baste the sides and the ends together with the cotton crochet thread. Fold the large rectangle in half lengthwise and baste the sides and the ends together with the cotton crochet thread. Felt in the washer until fully felted. Each color section should be about 10½"/27cm long and the rectangle will be about 18"/46cm wide. Remove the cotton crochet thread and let dry.

cutting the pattern pieces

Enlarge the patterns onto graph paper as shown in figure 1 and cut out. Lay out the pieces on the felted fabric as shown in figure 2 (you don't have to worry about having the pieces on the straight grain) or arrange them as desired. Cut out each piece, adding a ¼"/6mm seam allowance. Cut the lining pieces from the lining fabric, again adding a ¼"/6mm seam allowance.

front zippered pocket

Pin the zipper RS down on the WS of the front section, centered about 2½"/6cm down from the top edge. Use a zipper foot to stitch around all the edges. Turn over and use sharp scissors to cut a slit along the center of the stitching for the zipper opening. Pin the RS of the pocket lining to the WS of the front and stitch all around the front, ¼"/6mm from the edges. Cut the lining very close to the sewing line. (The steps in this segment are illustrated in figure 3.)

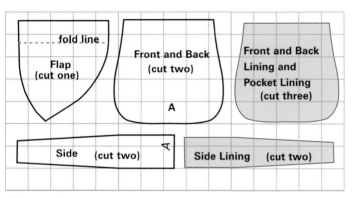

Figure 1. One square= 2"/5cm

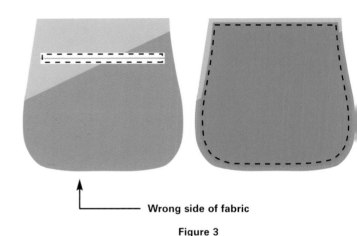

Wrong side of fabric

Figure 3

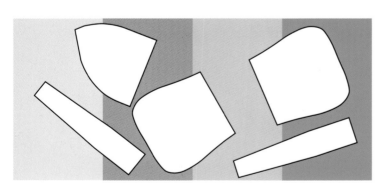

Figure 2

purse assembly

Refer to figure 4: Make a lapped seam to sew the sides together at the wide end, overlapping the edges ½"/13mm and stitching ¼"/6mm from each edge. Pin the front to the side section, WS tog, matching A at the center bottom. Sew together using ¼"/6mm seam allowance. Rep to sew the sides to the back. Overlap the flap over the back ½"/13mm and topstitch ¼"/6mm from the edges.

figure 5, RS facing. Turn the top edge ½"/13mm over to the outside (WS) of the lining and press. Slide the lining inside the purse, WS tog, and pin along the top edge. Slipstitch the lining in place along the top edge.

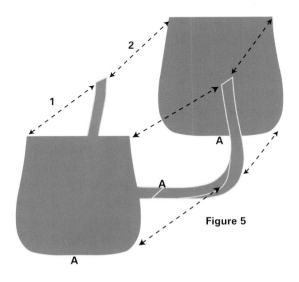

Figure 5

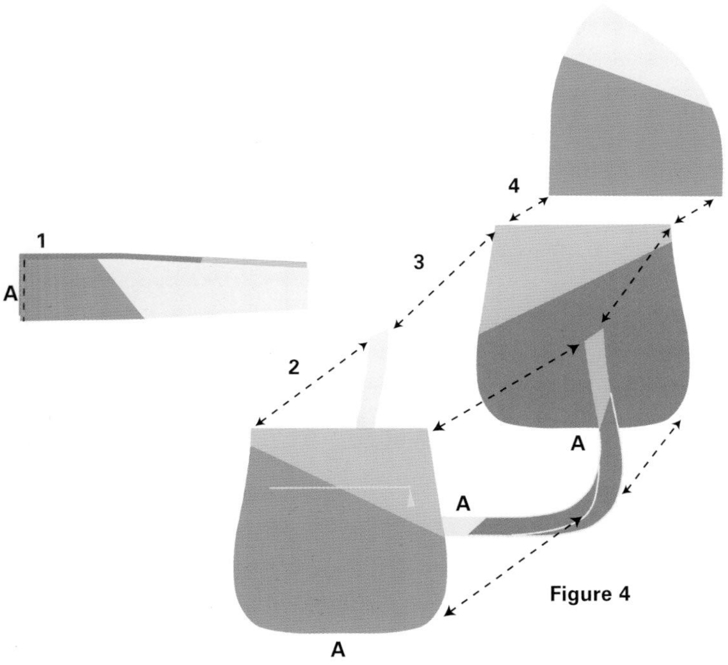

Figure 4

lining

Cut a 3 x 20"/8 x 51cm strip of lining fabric and fold the long edges under so the lining is about ⅛"/3mm narrower than the felted strap. Pin the WS of the lining to the WS of the strap and stitch the lining to the strap ¼"/6mm from ea edge, leaving the ends open. Overlap the strap ½"/13mm over the ends of the side sections of the bag and topstitch ¼"/6mm from the edges. Sew the lining side pieces tog as for the felted bag, and then sew the lining pieces together as in

this project was knit with

Dale of Norway's *Heilo*, 100% pure wool, sport weight, 1.75oz/50g = approx 109yd/100m per ball

(A) 2 balls, color #9331

(B) 2 balls, color #9834

(C) 2 balls, color #2427

(D) 2 balls, color #3152

colorwork

Bold designs and strong contrasts are the best ingredients for successful colorwork in felted knitting. Small infusions of color can blend and change appearance in the felting process; this can be a delightful surprise…or a disappointing revelation. Remember that much of the joy of felting your knitting lies in the experimentation, because you can learn just as much from the so-called failures as the successes.

The projects in this section demonstrate some entertaining ways to add colorwork to the knits you felt. In the vest on the following page, white yarn used in a stripe pattern blends with the adjoining colors to create a new shade. In the miniature rug on page 89, the white yarn hardly felts at all and thus is distinct from the rest of the pattern. Several projects display the use of changes within the colorwork pattern, including the additions of subtle hand-dyed yarn as well as the inclusion of variegated yarn. Because these projects include the use of stripes as well as colorwork following a chart, they are best suited to knitters with experience in these techniques.

This really easy vest is knit from side to side, felted completely, then cut to shape. Add an I-cord tie and you're done! During the felting process, the narrow white and green stripes blend to add a new color to the mix. It's a great technique to take advantage of because you get more color with less yarn.

finished measurements
of basted bodice

before felting
 Approx 19 (21, 24, 27, 30, 33, 36) x 25 (26, 27, 29, 30, 31, 33)"/48 (53, 61, 69, 76, 84, 91) x 64 (66, 69, 74, 76, 79, 84)cm

after felting
 Approx 13 (15, 17, 19, 21, 23, 25) x 18 (19, 20, 21, 22, 23, 24)"/33 (38, 43, 48, 53, 58, 64) x 46 (48, 51, 53, 56, 58, 61)cm

measurements of finished garment

size	chest	bodice length
Child S	26"/66cm	18"/48cm
Child M	30"/76cm	19"/48cm
XS/Child L	34"/86cm	20"/51cm
S	38"/97cm	21"/53cm
M	42"/107cm	22"/56cm
L	46"/117cm	23"/58cm
XL	50"/127cm	24"/61cm

yarn

Approx total: 1101 (1101, 1349, 1349, 1473, 1473, 1597)yd/1020 (1020, 1250, 1250, 1365, 1365, 1480)m wool sport weight yarn

Color A: 620 (620, 744, 744, 868, 868, 992)yd/575 (575, 690, 690, 805, 805, 920)m in white

Color B: 124 (124, 248, 248, 248, 248, 248)yd/115 (115, 230, 230, 230, 230, 230)m in blue

Color C: 248yd/230m in green

Color D: 109yd/100m in peach

materials

Knitting needles: 4.5mm (size 7 U.S.) *or size to obtain gauge*

3.5mm (size 4 U.S.) dpn for the I-cord

Cotton crochet thread

Tapestry needle and thread to match yarn color

gauge before felting

19 sts and 24 rows = 4"/10cm in Stockinette Stitch
Always take time to check your gauge.

pattern stitch

Stockinette Stitch

INSTRUCTIONS

rectangle for vest

CO 120 (124, 130, 140, 144, 148, 158) sts in A. Work in St st throughout.

Work 20 (25, 30, 37, 42, 47, 54) rows A, 2 rows B, 2 rows C, 2 rows A, 2 rows C, 2 rows D, 2 rows C, 2 rows A, 2 rows C, 2 rows B.

Work the foll rep 5 times:

20 (23, 29, 34, 40, 46, 51) rows A, 2 rows B, 2 rows C, 2 rows A, 2 rows C, 2 rows D, 2 rows C, 2 rows A, 2 rows C, 2 rows B.

Knit 20 (25, 30, 37, 42, 47, 54) rows in A, BO, weave in ends.

i-cord ties

Using A and dpn, make two 9"/23cm 3-stitch I-cords for the ties at the center front. Do not felt. Set aside.

felting

Fold the rectangle so the ends meet in the center front. Sew one of the sides together with A (this will be the shoulder seam). Baste the ends and other sides together with the cotton crochet thread. Felt in the washer. Remove the basting stitches and let dry.

assembly

Cut the armholes and neck opening, following the diagram in figure 1. To make sure the armholes are the same, cut one, then use it as a template for the other side. Try the vest on and adjust as needed, cutting more if necessary. Sew the 9"/23cm I-cords to the center front of the right and left.

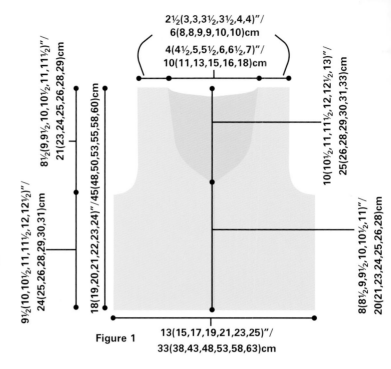

2½(3,3,3½,3½,4,4)"/
6(8,8,9,9,10,10)cm

4(4½,5,5½,6,6½,7)"/
10(11,13,15,16,18)cm

8½(9,9½,10,10½,11,11½)"/
21(23,24,25,26,28,29)cm

10(10½,11,11½,12,12½,13)"/
25(26,28,29,30,31,33)cm

9½(10,10½,11,11½,12,12½)"/
24(25,26,28,29,30,31)cm

18(19,20,21,22,23,24)"/45(48,50,53,55,58,60)cm

8(8½,9,9½,10,10½,11)"/
20(21,23,24,25,26,28)cm

Figure 1

13(15,17,19,21,23,25)"/
33(38,43,48,53,58,63)cm

this project was knit in child size small with

Dale of Norway's *Tuir*, 100% pure wool, sport weight, 1.75oz/50g = approx 124yd/115m per ball

(A) 5 balls, color White #0020

(B) 1 ball, color Blue #6222

(C) 2 balls, color Light Green #8533

Dale of Norway's *Heilo*, 100% pure wool, sport weight, 1.75oz/50g = approx 109yd/100m per ball

(D) 1 ball, color Peach #3102

native
american-style rug

White yarn is typically avoided for felting projects because the bleaching chemicals used to prepare it also prevent it from felting. It's true that the white yarn in this project hasn't felted as much as the other colors. But it actually enhances this design by keeping the edges crisp; otherwise they would have blended together and lost their definition. Use the effects of any yarn to your advantage.

finished measurements

before felting
  Approx 12 x 22"/30 x 56cm
after felting
  Approx 9½ x 18"/24 x 46cm

yarn

Approx total: 944yd/864m wool or wool blend worsted weight yarn

Color A: 184yd/168m of sport weight, wool, in beige

Color B: 190yd/174m of worsted weight, wool/mohair blend, in red

Color C: 190yd/174m of worsted weight, wool/mohair blend, in black

Color D: 190yd/174m of worsted weight, wool/mohair blend, in white

Color E: 190yd/174m of worsted weight, wool/mohair blend, in off white

materials

Knitting needles: 5.5mm (size 9 U.S.) *or size to obtain gauge*

Tapestry needle

gauge before felting

15 sts and 20 rows = 4"/10cm in Stockinette Stitch using worsted weight yarn

Always take time to check your gauge.

pattern stitch

Stockinette Stitch

note

Two strands of A held tog as one throughout.

INSTRUCTIONS

Work in St st throughout.

With E, CO 45 sts. Work 2 rows E, 8 rows A, 2 rows C, 4 rows B.

Follow the chart in figure 1 for the colorwork section.

Work 4 rows B, 2 rows C, 8 rows A, 2 rows E.

BO, weave in ends.

felting

Felt in the washer. Pull into shape if necessary and dry flat.

this project was knit with

Brown Sheep's *Nature Spun*, 100% wool, sport weight, 1.75oz/50g = approx 184yd/168m per ball

(A) 1 ball, color Latte #N93

Brown Sheep's *Lamb's Pride*, 85% wool/15% mohair, worsted weight, 4oz/113g = approx 190yd/174m per ball

(B) 1 ball, color Raspberry #M-83

(C) 1 ball, color Onyx #5

(D) 1 ball, color White #11

(E) 1 ball, color Oatmeal #115

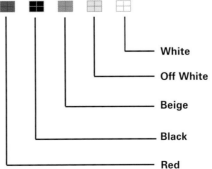

White

Off White

Beige

Black

Red

Figure 1

ruffled pillow

Beautiful stripes of hand-dyed yarn give this pillow an elegant touch. It's an adventure to make because you just throw the pillow in the washer and see how it shrinks!

finished measurements

before felting
  Ruffle: Approx 3"/8cm wide
  Pillow: Approx 14 x 16"/36 x 41cm

after felting
  Ruffle: Approx 2"/5cm wide
  Pillow: Approx 12"/31cm square

yarn

Approx total: 380yd/348m wool blend worsted weight yarn

Color A: 190yd/174m wool/mohair blend in pink

Color B: 190yd/174m wool/mohair blend in pale pink

materials

Knitting needles: 6mm (size 10 U.S.) 32"/81cm circular *or size to obtain gauge*

1yd/1m of worsted weight waste yarn

5mm (size H U.S.) crochet hook

4 stitch markers

Needle and thread to match fabric

Two 11 x 13"/28 x 33cm pieces of fabric for pillow back

Sewing machine

Tapestry needle

12"/31cm square pillow form

gauge before felting

14 sts and 22 rows = 4"/10cm in Stockinette Stitch
Always take time to check your gauge.

pattern stitch

Stockinette Stitch

INSTRUCTIONS

pillow front

With the waste yarn and crochet hook, ch at least 50 sts.

Using A, pick up 50 sts working into the back loops of the ch sts. Working in St st, work 5 rows in A, *2 in B, 2 in A, 2 in B, and 6 in A, rep from * 5 more times for a total of 6 reps, plus the 1st 5 rows and CO row.

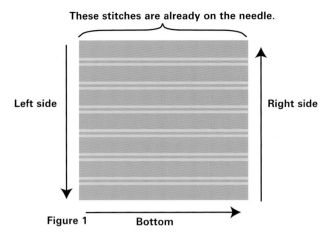

These stitches are already on the needle.

Left side

Right side

Figure 1   Bottom

ruffle

See figure 1. Using B and beg along the left side of the knitting, pick up one st along the side at the end of every other row, pm at end of side—39 sts.

Unraveling the crochet ch as you go, *k3 sts along the bottom, k2tog, rep from * across the bottom of the knitting, pm—40 sts.

Working along the right side of the knitting, pick up 1 st along the side at the end of every other row, pm—39 sts.

Working across the top row *k3, k2tog, rep from * to end of row, pm—40 sts. You will have 158 sts around.

Work 8 rnds in St st, k into the front and back of the st before and after the stitch marker in ea rnd. You will have 222 sts after 8 rnds.

On the next rnd, k into the front and back of ea st, removing all the stitch markers except the one that marks the beg of the rnd—444 sts.

Work 1 rnd even.

Continuing even, work 1 rnd in B, 1 in A, 2 in B, and 1 in A. BO in A, weave in ends.

felting

Felt in the washer, checking occasionally. Lay flat to dry, adjusting the pillow section into a square if necessary and arranging the ruffle into wavy curves around the pillow. Let dry.

assembly

Fold the fabric pieces over 3"/8cm along one of the 13"/33cm sides. Press. Fold the raw edge under ½"/13mm and stitch in place. This will be the center opening on the pillow back. Turn remaining raw edges of both pieces of fabric under ½"/13mm and press in place. Lay pieces on a table and overlap the centers, adjusting until pieces form a 12"/31cm square. Pin together at the overlapped section. Pin the back to the WS of felted pillow and hand sew in place along the edge of the pillow, leaving the ruffle free. Stuff the pillow form inside.

this project was knit with

Lorna's Laces' *Bullfrogs and Butterflies*, 85% wool/15% mohair, worsted weight, 3.5oz/100g = approx 190yd/174m per hank
(A) 1 hank, color Pink Blossom #1ns
(B) 1 hank, color Pale Pink #29ns

beautiful yarn bowl

This thick bowl made of yarn is designed *for* yarn. It's quick to knit using large needles and two, three, or four strands of yarn held together as one. This makes the bowl sturdy enough to hold your yarn, yet still flexible and lightweight. Note the effect of holding two different-color strands of yarn as one in the section just before the charted colorwork; it's a technique in and of itself.

finished measurements

before felting
Approx 18"/46cm diameter at widest section, 9½"/24cm diameter at opening

after felting
Approx 14"/36cm diameter at widest section, 11"/28cm diameter at opening, and 7"/18cm high
Note that the opening stretches as it felts.

yarn

Approx total: 1900yd/1740m wool blend worsted weight yarn

Color A: 380yd/347m in brown

Color B: 380yd/347m in wine

Color C: 190yd/174m in turquoise

Color D: 190yd/174m in purple

Color E: 190yd/174m in green

Color F: 190yd/174m in red

Color G: 190yd/174m in black

Color H: 190yd/174m in blue

materials

Knitting needles: 10mm (size 15 U.S.) dpn *or size to obtain gauge*

10mm (size 15 U.S.) 24"/61cm circular and 39"/99cm circular

8mm (size 11 U.S.) 32"/81cm circular

Tapestry needle

Stitch markers

gauge before felting

9 sts and 13 rows = 4"/10cm in Stockinette Stitch, holding four strands tog as one and using the 10mm (size 15 U.S) needles.

Always take time to check your gauge.

pattern stitches

Stockinette Stitch

K1 P1 Rib Stitch

INSTRUCTIONS

Holding 2 strands of A and 2 strands of B tog as one, CO 6 sts, 2 on ea of 3 dpn needles, pm.

Working in the round, k into the front and back of ea st—12 sts.

On the next round, *k into the front and back of the next st, k the next st, rep from *—18 sts.

On the next round, *k into the front and back of the next st, k the next two sts, rep from *—24 sts.

Cont, inc 6 sts ea rnd, changing to the 24"/61cm circular needle then the 39"/99cm needle to accommodate the increasing number of stitches. When you have 120 sts around (20 sts in each rep section) beg working even without inc.

Work 1 rnd even.

Change 1 strand of A to C and work three rnds even.

Change rem strand of A to C and work 3 rnds even.

Begin colorwork section, following chart in figure 1, using two strands of yarn for each color. After 7 rnds of the chart, change to 8mm (size 11 U.S.) needles and work 2 rnds of D.

Work k1, p1 rib for 4 rnds, knitting in 2 strands of F and purling in 2 strands of D.

Change to H and *k2tog, k2, rep from *.

Work 8 more rnds of H even in St st, BO, weave in ends.

felting

Felt in the washer, checking occasionally, until the bowl is thickly felted. Shape to a round bowl, letting the top edge curl over on itself to form a thick rim. Let dry.

this project was knit with

Brown Sheep's *Lamb's Pride*, 85% wool/15% mohair, worsted weight, 4oz/113g = approx 190yd/174m

(A) 2 balls, color Roasted Coffee #M-89

(B) 2 balls, color Chianti #M-28

(C) 1 ball, color Blue Heirloom #M-75

(D) 1 ball, color Amethyst #M-62

(E) 1 ball, color Limeade #M-120

(F) 1 ball, color Raspberry #M-83

(G) 1 ball, color Onyx #M-05

(H) 1 ball, color Blue Boy #M-79

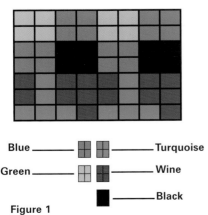

Blue ——— Turquoise
Green ——— Wine
——— Black

Figure 1

navy zigzag bag

This bright and bold bag features a sturdy garter stitch bottom and decorative straps—tapering to easy-to-hold handles made of I-cord—that attach firmly to the bag. The use of variegated yarn for the colorwork pattern adds visual interest to an otherwise simple collection of zigzags, stripes, and checkerboard motifs.

finished measurements of bag
(excluding straps)
before felting
  Approx 20 x 15"/51cm x 38cm
after felting
  Approx 15 x 11"/38cm x 28cm

yarn
Approx total: 490yd/448m wool worsted weight yarn

Color A: 164yd/150m in dark brown

Color B: 164yd/150m in navy blue

Color C: 81yd/74m in variegated orange shades

Color D: 81yd/74m in variegated blue shades
Scrap worsted weight yarn that contrasts with brown

materials
Knitting needles: 6mm (size 10 U.S.) 32"/81cm circular *or size to obtain gauge*

5.5mm (size I U.S.) crochet hook

Cotton crochet thread

Tapestry needle

Stitch marker

gauge before felting
15 sts and 19 rows = 4"/10cm in Stockinette Stitch
Always take time to check your gauge.

pattern stitches
Garter Stitch
Stockinette Stitch

INSTRUCTIONS
bottom of bag
Using the scrap yarn and crochet hook, loosely ch 45 sts, pull yarn through last loop. With A, CO 45 sts into the back loops of the ch. Work 32 rows in g st.

body of bag
Pick up sts the rest of the way around the bottom of the bag to begin knitting in the rnd: pick up 15 sts along one side of the knitting, unravel the contrasting yarn ch sts as you pick up the 45 sts along the CO row, pick up 15 sts along the other side, pm—120 sts. Working in St st in the rnd, work 6 rnds of A, then 4 rnds of B. Follow the chart in figure 1 for the

colorwork section. Then work 4 rnds of B, 4 rnds of D, 2 rnds of B and 1 rnd of A, p the next rnd in A, BO, and weave in ends.

handle (make two)

With D, CO 1 st.

Row 1 and all odd numbered rows until the I-cord section: P.

Row 2: K into the front and back of the st—2 sts.

Row 4: K into the front and the back of ea st—4 sts.

Row 6: K into the front and back of the 1st st, k to the last st, k into the front and back of the last st—6 sts.

Rows 7–10: Rep rows 5 and 6—8 sts, 10 sts.

Rows 11–13: Work even in St st.

Row 14 and Row 16: K2tog, k to last 2 sts, k2tog—8 sts, 6 sts.

Work even in St st for 15 more rows.

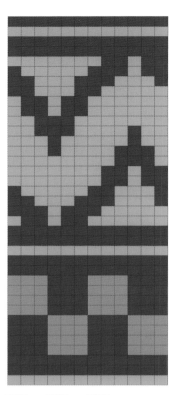

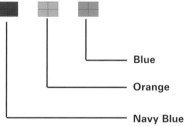

Blue

Orange

Navy Blue

Figure 1

On next row rep Row 14—4 sts.

Work 4-stitch I-cord for 20 rows.

P the next row.

On next row rep Row 6—6 sts.

Work even in St st for 15 more rows.

On the next 2 RS rows, rep Row 6—8 sts, 10 sts.

Work 3 rows even in St st.

On the next 3 RS rows, rep Row 14—8 sts, 6 sts, 4 sts.

On the next RS row, k2tog twice.

On the next RS row, k2tog, BO, weave in ends.

assembly

Sew the straps to the bag, placing the points of the strap ends along the top row of C stripe (the top row of the colorwork chart in figure 1). See the photo for general placement.

felting

Using the cotton crochet thread, sew the top edge of the bag closed and sew the straps together up to the I-cord section.

Felt, checking often to make sure the straps do not get caught and stretch. Be sure the bag is felting evenly. When fully felted, remove the cotton crochet thread from the top edge and the straps. Adjust the bag to the desired finished shape and let dry.

this project was knit with

Brown Sheep's *Waverly Wool*, 100% Persian wool, worsted weight, 4oz/112g = approx 164yd/150m per ball

(A) 1 ball, color Dark Brown #1211

(B) 1 ball, color Dark Blue #7121

Brown Sheep's *Waverly Wool*, variegated, 100% Persian wool, worsted weight, 2oz/57g = approx 81yd/74m per ball

(C) 1 ball, color Fall Colors #W8500

(D) 1 ball, color Ocean Treasures #W8300

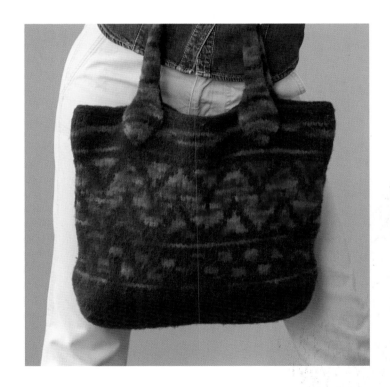

mixed
media

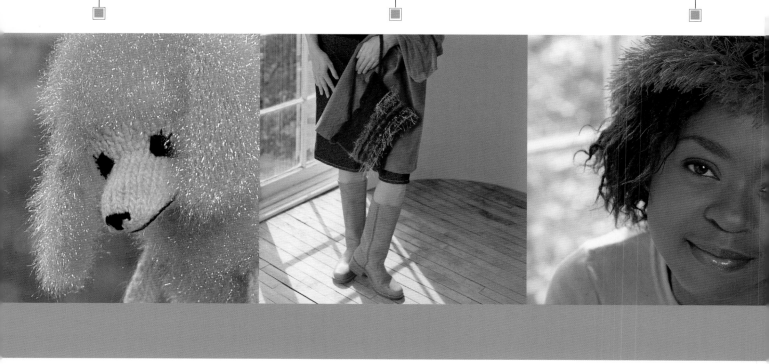

What a lot of fun to add novelty yarn to your felted knitting! The fuzzy or bumpy yarn fluffs out while the wool yarn shrinks. If you hold both yarns together as one when you knit, the whole piece will shrink down during felting and the novelty yarn will pop out. However, if you knit the novelty yarn on some rows and the wool yarn on others, the width of the piece will stay the same after felting. This is a convenient effect to use when designing a vest, since you only need to plan for the amount of vertical shrinkage that happens during the felting process.

experience level

easy ●

This wavy pattern is fun to knit, easy to felt, and great to touch. The novelty yarn keeps the felted section light and airy. Folding the piece in half and basting it together results in a scarf that's narrow in the middle and wider at the ends.

finished measurements

before felting
  Approx 13 x 58"/33 x 147cm

after felting
  Approx 11½"/29cm wide at center, 15"/38cm wide at ends, and 48"/122cm long

yarn

Approx total: 350yd/317m wool worsted weight yarn and eyelash yarn

Color A: 240yd/216m of eyelash yarn, polyester, in turquoise

Color B: 110yd/101m of worsted weight yarn, wool, in blue

materials

Knitting needles: 8mm (size 11 U.S.) *or size to obtain gauge*

Cotton crochet thread

Tapestry needle

gauge before felting

13 sts and 17 rows = 4"/10cm in Pattern Stitch

Always take time to check your gauge.

INSTRUCTIONS

Using A, CO 56 sts.

Rows 1–2: Working in A, k.

Row 3: K1, (k2tog) 3 times, [(k into front and back of next st) 6 times, (k2tog) 6 times] twice, (k into front and back of next st) 6 times, (k2tog) 3 times, k1.

Rows 4–5: K.

Change to B.

Row 6: P.

Row 7: Rep row 3.

Repeat rows 6–7 four more times—8 rows.

Row 16: P.

Rep rows 1–16 nine more times.

Rep rows 1–4. BO, weave in ends.

assembly

Fold the scarf so it's half as long and baste the sides tog with the cotton crochet thread. Leave the ends open.

felting

Felt in the washer, checking occasionally, until the wool yarn in the scarf is felted. Remove the cotton crochet thread and hang the scarf to dry.

this project was knit with

Lion Brand Yarn's *Fun Fur*, 100% polyester eyelash, 1.75oz/50g = approx 60yd/54m per ball
(A) 4 balls, color Turquoise #148

Lion Brand Yarn's *Fishermen's Wool*, 100% wool, worsted weight, 4oz/112g = approx 110yd/101m per ball
(B) 1 ball, color Blue #735

fifi the fluffy poodle

experience level

intermediate

Could there be a better stuffed animal to display the effects of felting and novelty yarn than a chichi pink poodle? Fifi is made of I-cord and easy tubes.

finished measurements
after felting
   Approx 15 x 12"/38 x 30 cm, including head and legs

yarn
Approx total: 338 yd/333m novelty yarn and wool blend worsted weight yarn

Color A: 148yd/160m of novelty yarn in pink

Color B: 190yd/173m of worsted weight yarn, wool/mohair blend, in pink

materials
Knitting needles: 5.5mm (size 9 U.S.) dpn *or size to obtain gauge*

Tapestry needle

Size 10 cotton embroidery thread for basting

Polyester fiberfill

Size 3 cotton embroidery thread, black and white, for the poodle's face

Beads and thread to make necklace and bracelet (optional)

gauge before felting
16 sts and 20 rows = 4"/10cm in Stockinette Stitch

Always take time to check your gauge.

pattern stitch
Stockinette Stitch

INSTRUCTIONS
head
With B, CO 10 sts. Working in St st, inc 1 st ea end every right side row until you have 18 sts. On the next RS row, inc 1 every other st—27 sts.

Work 4 rows even.

Change to A and work 1 row even.

On the next row, inc 1 every 3rd st—36 sts.

Work 1 row even.

On the next row, inc every 6th st—42 sts.

Work 1 row even.

On the next row, inc every 7th st—48 sts.

Work even for 5 rows.

Dec rows:

Row 1: (Dec 1, k6) rep 6 times—42 sts.

Beg working in the round.

(Dec 1, k5) rep 6 times—36 sts.

Continue decreasing 6 sts every round until there are 6 sts left. Weave through the 6 rem sts, baste opening closed with size 10 embroidery thread.

body

With A, CO 6 sts evenly on 3 dpn. Work in the rnd.

Rnd 1: K.

Rnd 2: Inc 1 ea st around—12 sts.

Rnd 3: K.

Rnd 4: (Inc 1 st, k next st) rep 6 times around —18 sts.

Rnd 5: K.

Rnd 6: (Inc 1 st, k 2 sts) rep 6 times around—24 sts.

Continue increasing 6 sts every other rnd until there are 96 sts.

Work even for 12 rnds.

Change to B and work 2 rnds, then work back and forth for 16 rows, then work in the rnd for 10 rnds. Dec evenly 6 times every other rnd until there are 12 sts left. Weave through rem 12 sts. Baste opening closed with size 10 cotton embroidery thread.

legs (make four)

With B, CO 6 sts on 3 dpn.

Work 4 rnds.

Change to A and work 1 rnd.

On the next rnd, inc 1 ea st—12 sts.

Work even for 4 rnds.

On the next rnd dec 1, rep around—6 sts.

Change to B and work 18 rnds. BO. Weave in ends.

ears (make two)

With A, CO 8 sts.

Work 8 rows in St st.

Dec 1st and last st on next 2 RS rows.

Work 2 rows even. BO, leaving a 10"/25cm tail to use to sew the ear to the head.

tail

With A, CO 6 sts on dpn.

Working in the rnd, inc 1 ea st—12 sts.

(Inc 1 st, k1) rep 6 times—18 sts.

Work 3 rows even.

(Dec 1, k1) rep 6 times—12 sts.

Stuff tail with fiberfill.

(Dec 1) rep 6 times—6 sts.

Change to B and work as I-cord for 8 rnds. BO.

felting

Felt all pieces *except* the ears in the washer until felted, being careful not to felt too long or the novelty yarn will get damaged. Let pieces dry.

embroidery

Remove the basting stitches from the head. Following figure 1, use stem stitch to stitch the mouth and use straight stitch for the eyes, nose, eyelashes, and white highlights in the eyes.

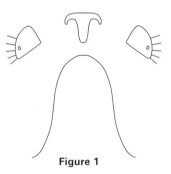

Figure 1

assembly

Remove the basting stitches from the body, stuff with fiberfill, and stitch the opening closed. Stuff the head with fiberfill and sew the opening closed. Using A, sew the head to the body and the ears to the sides of the head; using B, sew legs and tail to the body. Add optional jewelry as desired.

this project was knit with

Trendsetter Yarn's *Aura*, 100% nylon, worsted weight, 1.75oz/50g = approx 150yd/137m per skein

(A) 1 skein, color Bubblegum #7502

Lorna's Laces' *Bullfrogs and Butterflies*, 85% wool/15% mohair, worsted weight, 3.5oz/100g = approx 190yd/174m per hank

(B) 1 hank, color Pale Pink #29ns

experience level

easy

If you're ready to try adding novelty yarns to your felted knitting, here's the project for you. Make it as the instructions state, or just have fun changing from one yarn to the next and see what you come up with.

finished measurements

before felting
Approx 11 x 12"/28 x 30cm

after felting
Approx 11 x 8"/28 x 20cm

yarn

Approx total: 241yd/220m wool worsted weight yarn and novelty yarns

Color A: 218yd/199m of worsted weight yarn, wool, in purple

Color B: 3¼yd/3m of novelty yarn, ribbon, in purple

Color C: 3¼yd/3m of novelty yarn, bouclé, in lavender

Color D: 3¼yd/3m of novelty yarn, chenille, in variegated shades

Color E: 3¼yd/3m of novelty yarn, eyelash, in purple

Color F: 3¼yd/3m of novelty yarn, fur, in green

Color G: 3¼yd/3m of novelty yarn, bouclé, in purple

Color H: 3¼yd/3m of novelty yarn, eyelash, in green

materials

Knitting needles: 6.5mm (size 10.5 U.S.) 24"/61cm circular *or size to obtain gauge*

Tapestry needle

Stitch marker

Sewing needle and thread to match yarn color

8"/20cm zipper

gauge before felting

13 ½ sts and 18 rows = 4"/10cm in Stockinette Stitch

Always take time to check your gauge.

pattern stitches

Stockinette Stitch

K3 P3 Rib Stitch

INSTRUCTIONS

Using A, CO 75 sts, join into a circle, pm, and k in the rnd:

2 rnds A, 1 rnd B, 2 rnds A, 1 rnd C, 1 rnd A, 1 rnd with the remainder of B and finish rnd with D.

2 rnds A, 1 rnd E, 1 rnd A, 1 rnd with remainder of D and finish rnd with F.

4 rnds A, 1 rnd F, 3 rnds A, 1 rnd with remainder of F and finish rnd with G.

3 rnds A, 1 rnd holding A and H tog as one.

2 rnds A, 1 rnd with remainder of G ending with any remaining leftover novelty yarn and finishing with A.

Work rem rnds in A: 6 rnds in St st.

7 rnds in k3, p3 rib pat.

K 1 rnd.

Work the next rnd with a k and a p in every st— 150 sts.

K 2 rnds.

BO, weave in ends.

Make 4-stitch I-cord, 60 rows long.

felting

Sew bottom together with A. Use cotton crochet thread to baste top tog just below top ruffle. Fold I-cord in half and sew to corner of bag below ruffle. Felt in the washer, checking occasionally to make sure novelty yarns are not getting frayed. Remove basting thread and dry flat.

assembly

By hand, stitch each end of the opening together (below the ruffle) about 1 1/2"/4cm to accommodate the zipper. Sew the zipper to the inside of the bag. (If you'd rather, use an 11"/28cm zipper and eliminate stitching the sides.)

this project was knit with

Knit One, Crochet Too's *Parfait Solids*, 100% pure wool, worsted weight, 3.5oz/100g = approx 218yd/199m per ball

(A) 1 ball, color Eggplant #1730

K1C2's *Adornments*, variety pack of novelty fibers (B–H) 1 box, color Pansy

vest with zest

The use of the novelty yarn along the lower section keeps the felted fabric the same width after felting. This makes the vest certain to end up the correct width for your size. This project is quite simple to make, but it's a little time consuming.

finished measurements of tube

before felting
  Approx 17 (19, 21, 23, 25) x 25 (26, 27, 29, 31)"/43 (48, 53, 58, 64) x 64 (66, 69, 74, 79)cm

after felting
  Approx 17 (19, 21, 23, 25) x 20 (21, 22, 23, 24)"/43 (48, 53, 58, 64) x 51 (53, 56, 58, 61)cm

measurements of finished garment

size	chest	length
XS	34"/86cm	20"/51cm
S	38"/97cm	21"/53cm
M	42"/107cm	22"/56cm
L	46"/117cm	23"/58cm
XL	50"/127cm	24"/61cm

yarn

Approx total: 905 (905, 1140, 1140, 1358)yd/826 (826, 1040, 1040, 1239)m wool worsted weight yarn and novelty yarns

Color A: 872 (872, 1090, 1090, 1308)yd/796 (796, 995, 995, 1194)m of worsted weight yarn, wool, in tan
Color B: 6½ (6½, 10, 10, 10)yd/6 (6, 9, 9, 9)m of novelty yarn, eyelash, in brown
Color C: 6½ (6½, 10, 10, 10)yd/6 (6, 9, 9, 9)m of novelty yarn, ribbon, in brown
Color D: 6½ (6½, 10, 10, 10)yd/6 (6, 9, 9, 9)m of novelty yarn, eyelash, in iridescent
Color E: 6½ (6½, 10, 10, 10)yd/6 (6, 9, 9, 9)m of novelty yarn, ribbon, in variegated shades
Color F: 6½ (6½, 10, 10, 10)yd/6 (6, 9, 9, 9)m of novelty yarn, floss, in cream

materials

Knitting needles: 6.5mm (size 10.5 U.S.) 32"/81cm circular *or size to obtain gauge*

Tapestry needle

Stitch marker

Cotton crochet thread

4mm (size G U.S.) crochet hook

gauge before felting

16 sts and 18 rows = 4"/10cm in Stockinette Stitch
Always take time to check your gauge.

pattern stitch

Stockinette Stitch

INSTRUCTIONS

CO 136 (150, 168, 184, 200) sts. Join into a circle being careful not to twist the stitches, pm. Work in St st throughout.

Work 8 rnds A, 1 rnd B, 5 rnds A, 1 rnd C, 5 rnds A, 1 rnd D, 5 rnds A, 1 rnd E, 5 rnds A, 1 rnd F.

Continue in A until piece measures 25 (26, 27, 29, 31)"/64 (66, 69, 74, 79)cm total.

Fold tube so the center front is at the stitch marker. Graft tog at top for shoulders. Weave in all loose ends. Tie ends of specialty yarns tog in square knots. Baste bottom edge tog with cotton crochet thread.

felting

Felt in the washer until the fit is right, checking occasionally to make sure that the project hasn't felted too much and the novelty yarn hasn't frayed. Pull into shape if necessary and dry flat.

assembly

Remove the cotton crochet thread and cut the center front and armholes according to the dimensions shown in figure 1. To make the armholes the same size, cut one, then use the cutout section as a template to cut the other armhole. Using the crochet hook, sc along the front opening and neckline with A. Hand felt the armhole openings, using a brush to help the edges felt and fluff them out. Let dry.

this project was knit in size small with

Knit One, Crochet Too's *Parfait Solids*, 100% pure wool, worsted weight, 3.5oz/100g = approx 218yd/199m per ball

(A) 4 (4, 5, 5, 6) balls, color Tan #1893

K1C2's *Adornments*, variety pack of novelty fibers (B–F) 2 (2, 3, 3, 3) boxes, color Beige #AD10150

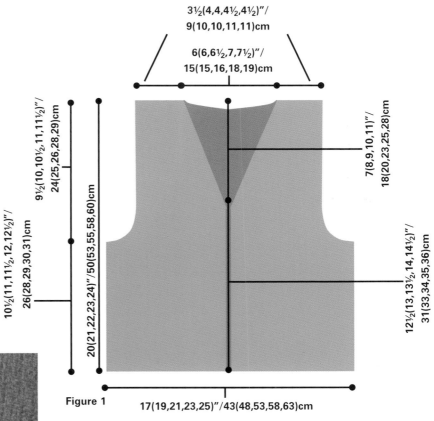

3½(4,4,4½,4½)"/ 9(10,10,11,11)cm

6(6,6½,7,7½)"/ 15(15,16,18,19)cm

9½(10,10½,11,11½)"/ 24(25,26,28,29)cm

7(8,9,10,11)"/ 18(20,23,25,28)cm

10½(11,11½,12,12½)"/ 26(28,29,30,31)cm

20(21,22,23,24)"/50(53,55,58,60)cm

12½(13,13½,14,14½)"/ 31(33,34,35,36)cm

Figure 1   17(19,21,23,25)"/43(48,53,58,63)cm

wildfire hat

This striking hat is the only novelty yarn project that has the felting yarn knitted throughout. The novelty yarn is carried along with the wool to create the stripes in the design. It's easy to make and fun to wear!

finished measurements

before felting
  Approx 13 x 12½"/33 x 32cm

after felting
  Approx 12" in diameter (22"/56cm in circumference)

yarn

Approx total: 283yd/258m wool worsted weight wool yarn and eyelash yarn

Color A: 223yd/204m of worsted weight yarn, wool, in black

Color B: 60yd/54m of eyelash yarn, polyester, in red

materials

Knitting needles: 8mm (size 11 U.S.) *or size to obtain gauge*

Tapestry needle

gauge before felting

13 sts and 17 rows = 4"/10cm in Garter Stitch
Always take time to check your gauge.

pattern stitch

Garter Stitch

INSTRUCTIONS

Holding A and B tog as one, CO 84 sts. Work in g st throughout.

K 4 rows.

*Change to A only and k 10 rows.

Change to A and B held tog as one and k 4 rows. Rep from * once.

K 10 more rows in A only.

Change to A and B and (k12, k2tog) 6 times—78 sts.

K the next row.

On the next row (k11, k2tog) 6 times—72 sts.

On the next row (k10, k2tog) 6 times—66 sts.

Continue color pat (10 rows A, 4 rows A and B, cutting and weaving in B each stripe), dec 6 sts ea RS row until you have 6 sts left.

K2tog 3 times.

Weave end through rem 3 sts.

assembly

Sew side seam with A. Weave in all loose ends.

felting

Felt, checking occasionally to make sure the hat doesn't shrink too much. When felted to the correct size, adjust the hat to desired finished shape and let dry.

this project was knit with

Patons' *Classic Merino Wool*, 100% pure new wool, worsted weight, 3.5oz/100g = 223yd/204m per ball
(A) 1 ball, color Black #226

Lion Brand Yarn's *Fun Fur*, 100% polyester eyelash, 1.75oz/50g = approx 60yd/54m per ball
(B) 1 ball, color Red #113

abbreviations

Approx approximately

beg begin(ning)

BO bind off

ch chain

cont continue

CO cast on

dec decrease

dpn double-pointed needle(s)

ea each

foll follow(s), following

g st garter stitch

inc increase

k knit

k2tog knit two together

k3tog knit three together

p purl

p2tog purl two together

pat pattern

pm place marker

rem remaining

rep repeat

rnd(s) round(s)

RS right side

sc single crochet

st(s) stitch(es)

St st stockinette stitch

tog together

WS wrong side

yo yarn over

glossary
of techniques

Here's a quick refresher course on some common knitting and sewing techniques that are used in the book.

backstitch. Strong utility stitch used to sew two pieces of fabric firmly together. The stitch is worked from right to left, creating long overlapped stitches on the back side of the fabric and a single line of stitches on the front. First, insert the needle from the wrong side. Make a stitch ¼"/6mm to the right, then come back through the fabric ½"/13mm to the left. Continue the line of stitching by inserting the needle ¼"/6mm to the right, meeting the previous stitch, and coming back through about ½"/13mm to the left.

bind off (BO). Working the last row of live stitches off the needle so they won't unravel. There are several techniques for this depending on the type of knitting you're doing.

■ *Basic bind off used in stockinette or garter stitch:* Knit two stitches, pass the first stitch on the right needle over the second stitch on the right needle. Knit the next stitch, pass the first stitch on the right needle over the second stitch on the right needle, and repeat until you've worked all the stitches across the row. Cut the yarn to about 6"/15cm and pull through the last stitch, weave in end.

■ *Binding off in pattern:* Work as for basic bind off above except knit and purl the stitches as you continue the pattern. For instance, in a knit one, purl one pattern you would knit the first stitch and purl the second stitch, then pass the

knit stitch over the purl stitch. Then you would knit the next stitch, pass the purl stitch over the knit stitch, purl the next stitch, and continue.

■ *Bind off when there are two or three stitches on the needle:* Cut the yarn to about 6"/15cm, thread with a tapestry needle and pass the yarn through the remaining stitches, weave in end.

buttonhole stitch. Variation of blanket stitch. This classic stitch is used for finishing edges around buttonholes (hence the name) and for fancy work such as crazy quilt stitches. With the needle through the buttonhole on the right side of the fabric, insert it about ⅛ to ¼"/6mm to 1.3cm away from the edge of the buttonhole, just a little to the right of where the thread is emerging. Holding the thread under the needle, pull until the thread is locked in a loop at the edge of the fabric. Repeat, making each stitch close to the previous one, and fanning the stitches slightly as you work around the corners of the buttonhole.

chain stitch. A classic embroidery stitch. Chain stitch is good to use when you want more definition than stem stitch provides. Begin by coming up through the fabric to the right side. Loop the thread around where you will make your stitch, insert the needle at the same point where the thread is coming out of the fabric and take a stitch as long as you want the chain to be, about 1/8 to 1/4"/6mm to 13mm. Pull the thread until the loop is snug. Repeat, placing each successive stitch within the loop of the previous chain.

colorwork. Generally speaking, this term means to knit following a chart, creating a pattern in which different colored yarns are used in the same row. You hold the yarn not in use on the wrong side of the knitting, knitting it only when needed. If the pattern has more than three or four stitches between colors, you must catch the yarn not in use as you knit a stitch with the working yarn. This step prevents long "floats" that will pull the knitting or hang loosely.

decrease (dec).
Knitting two stitches together as one (k2tog).

duplicate stitch. Duplicating the stitch pattern in the knitting by embroidering over it. To create the stitch, begin with the yarn coming out at the base of the loop of a stitch. Then pass the needle behind the stitch above, following the path of the stitch you're covering. Insert the needle at the base of the loop, covering the stitch with the embroidery thread. Pull the stitch so it is the same tension as the knitting. Repeat for each stitch.

edgestitch. Stitching by machine close to the edge of the fabric or fold, usually 1/8"/6mm or less.

garter stitch (g st). Knitting every stitch in every row. This pattern creates a bumpy horizontal stripe.

grafting. See **kitchener stitch**.

i-cord. Making a functional tube of knitting. Use two double pointed needles to work the stitches. (If you don't have the correct size double pointed needles you can use circular needles, though it's a little awkward to slide the knitting all the way to the other end of the circular.) Cast on three to five stitches and knit across. Keeping the right side of the knitting facing you, slide the stitches to the other end of the needle and pull the working yarn around the back of your work so you can knit the next row from right to left on the right side of the knitting. This creates the tube, which you can use for many different purposes, such as fringe, straps, or handles. You may need to pull the first stitch in each row a little tighter than the other stitches so they are all the same size when finished. To bind off the ends of I-cord, cut the working yarn to about 6"/15cm, thread it with a tapestry needle, and pass it through the last row of stitches. Weave the end into the I-cord.

increase (inc). Knitting into the front and the back of the stitch to increase one stitch.

joining finished edges. Two variations are used in this book, both utilizing whipstitch. If you are using the working yarn and want the seam to be permanently felted together, make the stitches close together; if you are temporarily basting the edges together with cotton embroidery thread, make the stitches longer so it's easier to remove them later. See also **whipstitch**.

kitchener stitch. Attaching two pieces of knitting by weaving their last row of live stitches together. Also called grafting, this technique creates an invisible seam because you're actually working a row of knitting to attach the two pieces together. It works invisibly in stockinette stitch and is half a stitch off on mixed pattern stitches. To begin, each piece should be on its last row on the needle. (You pull the stitches off the needle only as you finish weaving them together.) Lay the pieces flat on the table, one in front of the other. The needles should be horizontal and next to one another, the points both on the right side. The knit side of the fabric should be facing up; if necessary, knit an extra row on one piece so the needle points are both at the same end when the knitting is oriented as described. On the piece in front, closest to you, cut the working yarn to about three times the width of the knitting and thread it through a tapestry needle.

To graft in stockinette stitch, pass the tapestry needle through the first two stitches on the farthest piece, going in the first stitch from front to back and out the second stitch from back to front. Now pass through the first and second stitch on the piece closest to you in the same manner. Pull the first stitch of each piece off the needle, pulling the stitch you just made so its the same tension as the rest of the knitting. Repeat the process across the knitting, passing through the new first and second stitch on each needle, then pulling the first stitch off the needle. Weave in ends.

knit one, purl one rib (k1p1 rib).

Pattern that creates narrow vertical stripes. For items worked in the round you must have a multiple of two stitches, and you (knit one, purl one), repeating the pattern around and around. For flat items that have an odd number of stitches you (knit one, purl one) repeating across. On the next row you (purl one, knit one) repeating across. For flat items that have an even number of stitches, you (knit one, purl one) repeating across for every row.

knit two, purl two rib (k2p2 rib).

Pattern that creates wide vertical stripes. For items worked in the round you must have a multiple of 4 stitches, and you (knit two, purl two), repeating the pattern around and around. **Knit three, purl three rib** (k3p3 rib) creates wider stripes. It's worked as above with a multiple of six stitches.

mattress stitch. Seam used for the pieces in most knitted garments. (It should not be used in parts of projects that will be felted because it adds bulk to the finished piece.) Butt the edges of the two pieces together, right sides up. Use a tapestry needle to weave in and out of the running threads between the stitches on each side, about one stitch in from the edge. Pull the mattress stitches tight so the seam closes together, but not so tight that you pull the seam shorter than the rest of the knitted item. Repeat along the entire edge, pulling the stitch together every so often. Weave in ends.

seed stitch. Textural stitch. For items worked in the round you must have a multiple of two stitches plus one, and you (knit one, purl one), repeating the pattern around and around. For flat items that have an even number of stitches you (knit one, purl one) repeating across. On the next row you (purl one, knit one) repeating across. For flat items that have an odd number of stitches, you (knit one, purl one) repeating across for every row.

slipstitch. Worked with a crochet hook and cotton yarn to keep the edges of the knitting from distorting in the felting process. Insert the hook into the edge of the knitting, wrap the yarn around the hook, and pull through the knitting, (insert the hook

in the edge of the knitting about ¼"/6mm away, wrap the yarn around the hook, and pull through the knitting and the loop on the hook), repeat across the edge. You want your stitches to be fairly tight so that they are a strong support for the edge in the felting process. Remove the cotton yarn after felting.

stem stitch. Embroidery stitch for making lines. Working from left to right, begin with the thread coming through to the right side at your starting point. Take a stitch, inserting the needle about ½"/13mm away to the right and coming up about ¼"/6mm to the left. Repeat, always coming up on the same side of the stitch. The stitches on the right side of the fabric should be twice as long as the stitches on the underside of the fabric.

stockinette stitch (St st). Knitting every stitch on the right side of the knitting and purling every stitch on the wrong side of the knitting. This stitch creates a smooth even fabric and is a standard knitting pattern, probably the most common of all.

straight stitch. The basic flat stitch. **Satin stitch** is a group of straight stitches worked immediately adjacent to one another that cover an area with color.

weave in ends. Hiding all the loose ends of yarn. There are several methods used in this book.

▧ *Traditional yarn.* In knitting, you usually don't want any knots (see exception below). Cut all your tail ends at least 3 to 4"/8 to 10cm long, then thread them into a tapestry needle. Weave them in and out of the stitches for about 2"/5cm so they are hidden, then cut them close to the knitting. Be careful to keep the tension the same as the knitting so it

doesn't distort the fabric. Don't go back and forth over the same place while you're weaving or it will make the fabric thicker in that area.

▧ *Novelty yarn.* Many novelty yarns unravel or slide out of stitches if they are woven in using the traditional method described above. Since they are textured yarns, you can usually tie the ends in a square knot on the wrong side of the knitting and cut them about 1"/3cm long—they won't be noticeable.

▧ *Beading thread.* This material needs to be knotted before weaving in, and sometimes it needs to be knotted as you are working to hold the beads in place. Here's a quick and easy knot: take a small stitch close to where the thread exits the fabric, then pass through the loop you've created before you pull it tight.

whipstitch. Evenly spaced stitch that holds edges together. This stitch can be used two ways. The first is to baste knitting together before felting, using thread that you will pull out later; make these stitches far apart for easy removal.

The second is to use the working yarn and felt it into the finished piece. Make these stitches close together to join the pieces permanently. Place the finished edges side by side and weave the stitches in and out, joining the pieces but not creating a seam. This is the best method to use for finished edges that will be felted. Whipstitch is easy—take a small stitch through both pieces of knitting along the edge to be joined, then take another stitch ¼ to ½"/6mm to 13mm away. Repeat all along the edge.

templates

pink scarf, page 57

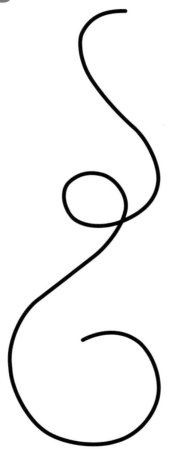

mola rug, page 68

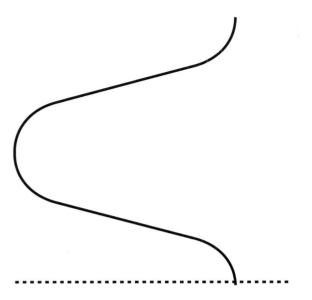

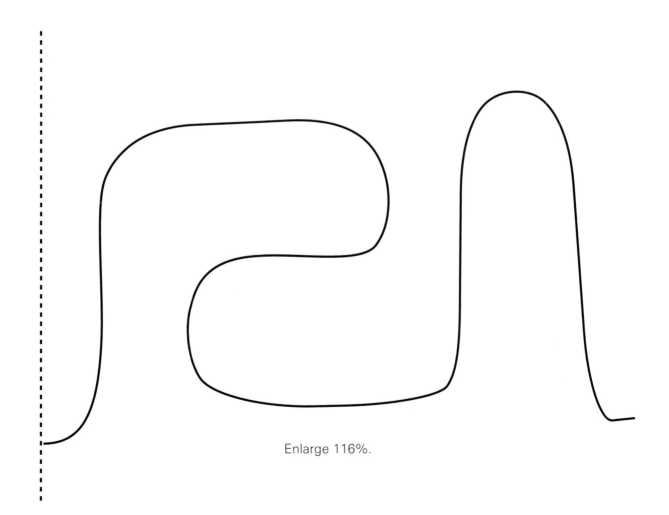

Enlarge 116%.

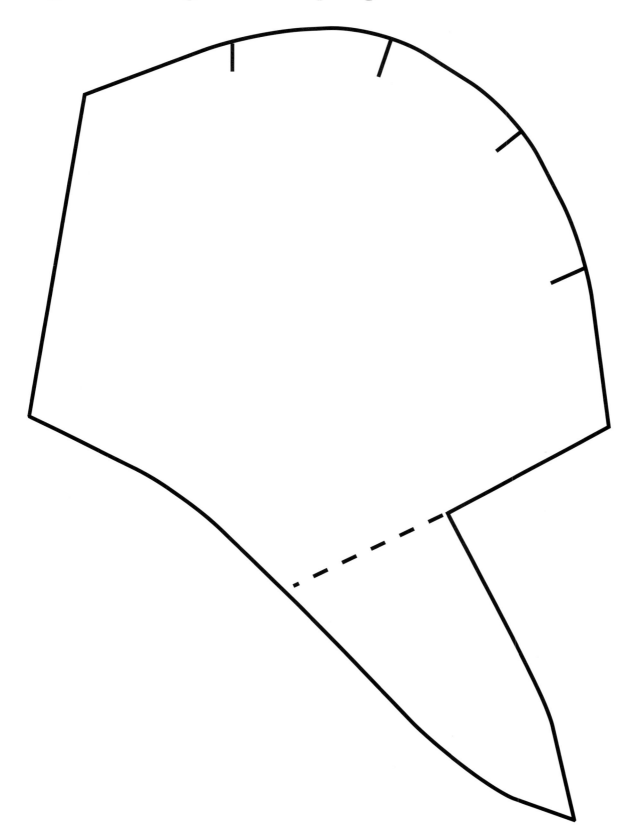

acknowledgments

Getting a book into print at Lark Books is always a collaboration between the author and the many talented people who work hard to create a quality product. I have several people to thank for working with me on this process.

Thank you so much to my fabulous editor, Valerie Shrader, who has been wonderful to work with, from the beginning deadlines that helped keep me on track to the thoughtful and thorough editing which made this book more complete with each pass. I look forward to working with you on future books.

Thank you to Marilyn Hastings for your technical expertise, which is indispensable in a knitting book.

Thank you to Tom Metcalf for your artful layout, the hallmark of a Lark book steeped in quality and style.

Thank you to Stewart O'Shields for the innovative and beautiful photography that brought these projects to life.

Thank you to the models: Franzi Charen, Victoria Fall, Megan Kirby, Janice Mompoint, Janna Norton, and Maria Wise, and the stylist who made them look so fabulous, Valerie Ingram. Special thanks to Ambiance Interiors/Sluder Furniture Company in Asheville, North Carolina, for the use of their facilities, and thanks for the boots from Belle Boutique, also of Asheville, North Carolina.

Thank you to Deborah Morgenthal for working with me at the beginning stages, especially when we were ironing out the projects and the look of the book.

A special thank you to Carol Taylor, for continuing to include me in Lark's adventures in books. It's an honor to be working with the creative team at Lark.

Thank you to the yarn companies who have provided the beautiful yarn for the projects in this book. It has been a joy working with these yarns as I explored the many possibilities of felting.

Here are the yarns that I used in this book:
Baabajoe's, *Wool Pak*
Brown Sheep, *Nature Spun*, *Lamb's Pride*, *Waverly Wool*
Cascade Yarns, *Cascade 220*
Classic Elite Yarns, *Paintbox*, *Two.Two*, *La Gran*, *Gatsby*, *Inca Alpaca*, *Wings*
Dale of Norway, *Heilo*, *Tuir*
Harrisville Designs, *New England Knitters Highland*, The *Orchid Line*
K1C2, *Adornments*
Knit One Crochet Too, *Parfait Solids*
Lion Brand Yarn, *Fun Fur*, *Fishermen's Wool*
Lorna's Laces, *Bullfrogs and Butterflies*
Mountain Colors, *4/8's Wool*
Patons, *Classic Merino Wool*
Reynolds Yarns, *Lopi*, *Lite-Lopi*, *Harmony*
Trendsetter Yarns, *Aura*

index

a note about suppliers

Usually, the supplies you need for making the projects in Lark books can be found at your local craft supply store, discount mart, home improvement center, or retail shop relevant to the topic of the book. Occasionally, however, you may need to buy materials or tools from specialty suppliers. In order to provide you with the most up-to-date information, we have created a list of suppliers on our website, which we update on a regular basis. Visit us at www.larkbooks.com, click on "Craft Supply Sources," and then click on the relevant topic. You will find numerous companies listed with their web address and/or mailing address and phone number.